VOLUME 1

| WOMEN |
| IN BUSINESS |

MISSION MATTERS

World's Leading Entrepreneurs Reveal their
TOP TIPS TO SUCCESS

ADAM TORRES AND
RANI KHETARPAL

Century City, CA

Listen to our
PODCASTS

MISSION **MATTERS**
WE AMPLIFY STORIES

www.MissionMatters.com

© 2020 Adam Torres. All rights reserved.

Copyright © 2020 by Mr. Century City, LLC. All rights reserved. No part of this book may be used or reproduced in any manner whatsoever without written permission except in the case of brief quotation embodied in critical articles and reviews.

For information, visit **www.MissionMatters.com**

Managing Editor:
Jyssica Schwartz

Graphic Design:
Kendra Cagle

Century City, CA 90067
www.MissionMatters.com

The Mr. Century City Logo is a trademark of Mr. Century City, LLC.

Mission Matters, Beverly Hills, CA

This publication is intended to provide general information regarding the subject matter covered. However, laws and practices often vary from state to state and are subject to change. Because each factual situation is different, specific advice should be customized to the particular circumstances. For this reason, the reader is advised to consult with his or her own adviser regarding that individual's specific scenario.

This book was created as a collaborative effort. Each author's opinion is solely their own. The authors have taken reasonable precautions in the preparation of this book and think the facts shown in the book are accurate as of the date it was written. However, neither the authors nor the publisher assumes any responsibility for any liability resulting from the use or application of the information contained in this book, and the information is not intended to serve as legal or professional advice related to individual situations.

DEDICATION

This book is dedicated to all of the women who are making an impact each and every day.

Raviya, that means you!

TABLE OF CONTENTS

Acknowledgments i
Foreword By Adam Torres iii
Introduction By Rani Khetarpal vii

CHAPTER 1: 1
**Emotionally Intelligent Wonder Women:
Behold Our SHEro Leadership Powers at Work**
By Dr. Airies Davis, Ed.D, MBA

CHAPTER 2: 15
Empathy - the Foundation of EQ
By Banu Raghuraman

CHAPTER 3: 25
Failing Into Success
By Camilla Jeffs

CHAPTER 4: 35
Authority Marketing 101
By Carolyn Barth, CEO, Digital Content Strategy LLC

CHAPTER 5: 43
Ready to Shine
by Claudia Romo Edelman

CHAPTER 6: 51
**Deal Sense™: How to Identify Opportunities,
Build Relationships, & Drive Value In Any Deal**
By Cydni Tetro

CHAPTER 7: 61
The Path to your Purpose: Directions and Decisions
By Denisa Axhami

CHAPTER 8: 69
Gnothi Seauton (Know Thyself): Lessons from a Global Music Producer
By Krystalán Chryssomallis

CHAPTER 9: 75
Turning Passion Into Your Purpose
By Dr. Lori Haddad

CHAPTER 10: 85
Getting Personal with Finance
By Marguerita Cheng

CHAPTER 11: 95
The Dream Job That Wasn't
By Marisa Impellizzeri

CHAPTER 12: 103
How to Turn Life's Challenges into Gifts: A Journey from Cancer Survivor to CEO
By Michelle Mekky

CHAPTER 13: 113
Iron Sharpening Iron
By Racquel Rivera

CHAPTER 14: 121
Implementing Value-Based Care for Cancer Patients
By Rani Khetarpal

CHAPTER 15: 135
How High is your EQ? The Case for Social Emotional Intelligence
By Renee Lopez-Cantera

CHAPTER 16: 149
The Big Three of Workplace Success: Differences, Diversity, and Decency
By Rita Kakati-Shah

CHAPTER 17: 155
Encouraging the Next Generation of Female Technology Leaders
By Shannon Wilkinson

CHAPTER 18: 165
Women in Business: Emotional Intelligence is the Underrated Skill of Success
By Victoria Sosa

Conclusion 173
Appendix.. 175
Listen to Our Podcasts 181
The Podcast Matters School........................ 183
Other Available Titles 187

ACKNOWLEDGMENTS

Thank you to Milos for your support - always.

Thank you to my girls for being my inspiration to want to always be better.

Thank you to my parents for all your lessons and examples, but most of all for showing me how to believe in myself and my brother for being the best example of "being the best" at what you do.

Thank you to Adam and Chirag at Mission Matters for this opportunity.

Thank you to all those who have been part of my personal and professional journey - I am blessed to have each and every one of you as part of my story.

FOREWORD

By **ADAM TORRES**

Whenever I'm interviewed, common questions I often get are: Who has had the biggest influence in your life? Who has been your most influential mentor? Who is your hero?

My answer is always the same: my mom.

I guess many of us think our moms are amazing, and rightfully they are, but I'll tell you a little more about my own mother and why she has had such a huge impact on my life.

My mom was a social worker for 40+ years before she eventually retired. During her career, she worked with some of the most at-risk youth in the country. From an early age, I remember having very adult conversations with her about what was going on in the community and how the choices we make can often lead to our success or failure. By providing real-life examples and not sheltering me from the sometimes harsh realities, she instilled in me a sense of resilience that has lasted me to this day.

Something else my mom gave me was a sense of how to build community. She didn't do this through preaching or telling me what to do and how to do it. She led by example. Some of my earliest memories are of going to events my mom put together for our community. Often, these events were a way to keep at-risk youth off the streets and doing something productive. Giving the community somewhere to belong and feel connected. Community advocates and organizers are big buzzwords nowadays, but she was doing that more than 30 years ago. Many times now, I'll read books and watch documentaries about building community and best practices and just have that jaw-dropping moment where I have to ask myself, "How did my mom know to do that before I was even born?" Whether it was intuitive or from training, I know that she has affected thousands of lives and has countless success stories of people she has helped.

Finally, my mom is a pioneer. Though she would never use those words herself, she was. As the second employee of Covenant House Michigan, she was part of bringing much-needed services to the at-risk youth of Michigan. A few quick stats about Covenant House: 1,968 kids on average sheltered nightly, over 10,200 kids cared for in their residential program, and nearly 74,000 kids reached in the past year. *(Numbers collected July 2018-June 2019. Visit https://www.covenanthouse.org/ for more information).*

I still remember when Dr. Sam Joseph hired her. Why is this memory vivid in my mind so many years later? Because she had me working for days to help move them into their new office. Ha! Let's just say my mom was the ultimate grass-roots organizer. She is definitely where I got my "can-do attitude" of getting the job done regardless of resources. She always led by example.

This brings me to the book that you are holding in your hands right now. This is a very special book for Mission Matters. It's our first Women in Business Edition. When my co-founder, Chirag Sagar, and I discussed the idea of creating a special series specifically for women, we weren't exactly sure how it would turn out. Meaning that, in publishing, you can do all of the research and have a great idea, but it doesn't mean anyone will necessarily care. However, we felt that this series was well worth the risk. Our aim with this new series is to provide a greater voice and platform for women from all backgrounds and walks of life to share their stories, their successes, and their expertise. For women like my mom, whose story may be lost in time if not written, archived, and shared in books like the one you are holding.

I'm not surprised, but definitely not claiming to have predicted this, but the content submitted for this book has been a great success. Each author shares insights and valuable lessons that I have benefited from both personally and professionally. I'm absolutely sure our readers will, too.

On that note, it's my honor to bring you the very first edition of our Women in Business series!

To your success,

Adam Torres

P.S. Visit **www.MissionMatters.com** to listen to more informative and inspirational stories.

INTRODUCTION

By **RANI KHETARPAL**

I always knew I wanted to be a mom. I wanted the whole thing actually: husband, kids, white picket fence, dogs, you know, the picture of perfection. But I also wanted a career and to rise to the top of my field. But "having it all" was not common and examples were difficult to find. No one ever talked about it; it was like wanting a family and a career was something never to be discussed. But if you looked around, even back then, there were examples of women doing just that. With little fanfare or accolades, they went about fulfilling their dreams. In fact, I had one example right in front of me. I didn't realize it at the time, but my mom, my biggest influencer growing up, did just that. Looking back, she was my first female role model of being successful in a male-dominated field - construction. My parents had their own custom home construction company, and while my dad worked his "day job" as an aerospace engineer, my mom ran the construction business - literally spending hours and hours at the construction site, managing workers and overseeing the process. She was a trained accountant with a master's degree, but there she was, a construction forewoman by day, mother and wife by night. I had zero appreciation for it then, but now I am in complete awe.

Without even knowing it, my mom was teaching me tenacity, perseverance, confidence, and grit. Her philosophy has always been to do what fuels you and be the best at it. Not "strive to be the best," just "be the best." Now as a mom of two teenage girls about to set foot in the real world, it is a message I continue to pass on to them every chance I get.

When I was growing up, I really wanted to be an actress. Then it was a corporate lawyer (I had no idea what that meant, it just sounded good), and finally, it was broadcast journalism. Nowhere in my formative years did I say I wanted to get into pharmaceuticals, be an entrepreneur, and dive into the business of healthcare. But that's how the cookie crumbled. As I dove into the world of business, the lessons I didn't even know I learned kicked in. Climbing the corporate ladder, I came to learn that women are often pitted against each other. We look enviously at successful women - however you choose to define that - and are automatically programmed to think that if we had all the advantages she has, then we, too, could be successful. Whether it's connections, money, family support, or even looks, the common phrase is "Well, she has that because…" It's a societal pressure to think that a woman's position is somehow tied to something other than her own skills and achievements. The mentality of jealousy and competition runs deep. I know - my younger self used to think this way.

But I have learned as I grew professionally and personally that judgment is counterproductive to not only women in general, but to one's own individual self. I have learned to celebrate the accomplishments of my fellow females and be proud that we are breaking ceilings through each and every goal that is accomplished. My narrative has evolved from "Why can't I do what she does?" to "Wow, that's amazing. I want to do what she is doing. How can I learn to do that?"

I have also realized, not in an easy way, that acceptance of one's self is crucial to how you embrace your journey.

I can't tell you how many times I have been dismissed for one superficial reason or another. I used to retreat when I knew I was being negatively judged. Over time, I realized I have no control over others' judgment of me, but I do have control over my reaction to it. Now, when this occurs, I rise up. I relish in proving the judgment wrong. I know I am competent, fierce, and can hold my own in any situation. I have learned that you do not have to lose yourself to be the executive or leader in your field you aspire to be. Quite the opposite; as soon as you embrace your true self, you find a confidence that cannot go unnoticed and shines from within.

Professionally, as my career evolved, I found myself heavily involved in trying to improve the process and business of healthcare delivery, specifically around post-acute care and oncology. I did not set out to be in this field, in this manner. You could say this is where fate and a little bit of luck stepped in. Yes, my family, like many of yours, has been affected by cancer. But this was not what I had set out to do, nor was it my primary motivation to get into the field. But my journey led me here, and as I got deeper into the world of cancer, so did my passion for finding ways to improve the cancer care journey for patients, caregivers, providers, and payers. There is so much work yet to be done, and sometimes it feels futile, but make no mistake, there is forward movement.

I am of the opinion that those who have been, are currently, or could be affected by cancer should be educated on the transition taking place in cancer care delivery. These changes are driving decision making, quality of care, and, ultimately, outcomes. Be assured these changes are absolutely a step in the right direction, but it is a work in progress. I decided to use this platform to write about these shifts in cancer care because I feel it is important enough and personal enough to me to be a voice and advocate for this positive transition. As such, you will learn more about the work currently in progress around cancer care delivery in my chapter. Cancer care is in the midst of an evolution, and I do feel very I privileged to be part of this change. My hope is that at least one person is informed and has a better patient experience because of the information provided in my chapter.

In addition to doctors, nurses, pharmacists, administrators, and other team members involved in the daily care of patients, the cancer community is supported by some amazing non-profit organizations. Some you probably are aware of, some you may not be. These organizations are vital in driving change that keeps the patient as the central point of focus. A passion that has been instilled in me as a child was the concept of giving back. As I dug deeper into the world of oncology, I became involved in some of the organizations truly on the front lines fighting the good fight each and every day. Currently, I am a regional board member for the American Cancer Society and serve on a national leadership council for Oncology Nurse Navigation. Two organizations that are serving the cancer community in different ways, but with similar missions - to improve the cancer journey for all those involved with the ultimate goal of making sure the patient journey is the central focus. I also volunteer my time around the community and with various professional and non-profit organizations. In addition, I am a Strategic Advisor and board member of Global Transitional Care, which is the company I founded and launched several years ago.

I am extremely honored to be a part of this first all-women edition of Mission Matters. Does being a woman make some things more difficult and present challenges? Yes, but it's far from being a barrier. As my mother so aptly demonstrated, with grit, determination, and hard work - and the willingness to persevere - no doubt success will follow. The women in this book are examples of exactly this. They have been on amazing journeys, and their stories and knowledge they share will show just how extraordinary women in business are.

Rani Khetarpal

CHAPTER 1

EMOTIONALLY INTELLIGENT WONDER WOMEN: BEHOLD OUR SHERO LEADERSHIP POWERS AT WORK

By **DR. AIRIES DAVIS, ED.D, MBA**

Have you ever dreamt of a workplace utopia where your SHEro (She-Hero) powers are respected and admired as symbols of effective leadership?

Hailed from the hidden Paradise Island of Amazonian warriors, DC Comics' superhero Wonder Woman is revered for her wisdom, strength, beauty, and agility. She even possesses the unique emotional capacity to detect all beings in a physically ostensible manner. Similar to this iconic SHEro's alter ego, Diana, oftentimes women leaders are not recognized for their emotional capacity at work. Seminal research from Daniel Goleman defines this capacity as emotional intelligence (EQ/EI) or the ability to 1) identify and manage your emotions, 2) manage and identify the emotions of others, and 3) build trust and grow influence. These abilities are derived from five domains of emotional intelligence: 1) Know your emotions, 2) manage your emotions, 3) motivate yourself, 4) recognize and understand the emotions of others, and 5) manage relationships or others' emotions.

Join me as we embark on a journey through the world of work in disguise as Wonder Woman. We will examine four displayed quadrants of superhero powers essential for emotionally intelligent women to effectively lead at work: self-awareness, self-management, social awareness, and relationship management.

Self-awareness refers to the ability to manage and recognize one's own emotions and their impact on decision-making. Self-management is the fortitude to control one's behaviors and emotions while exercising adaptability to change. Next, social awareness is the competencies to understand, sense, and respond to the emotions of others while feeling socially comfortable. And the final superpower identified as relationship management is one's ability to build connections, inspire, and influence others and manage conflicts.

		Recognition	Regulation
Personal Competence		**Self-Awareness** ✓ Self-confidence ✓ Awareness of your emotional state ✓ Recognizing how your behavior impacts others ✓ Paying attention to how others influence your emotional state	**Self-Management** ✓ Getting along well with others ✓ Handling conflict effectively ✓ Clearly expressing ideas and information ✓ Using sensitivity to another person's feelings (empathy) to manage interactions successfully
Social Competence		**Social Awareness** ✓ Picking up on the mood in the room ✓ Caring what others are going through ✓ Hearing what the other person is "really" saying	**Relationship Management** ✓ Getting along well with others ✓ Handling conflict effectively ✓ Clearly expressing ideas/information ✓ Using sensitivity to another person's feelings (empathy) to manage interactions successfully

Source: Roipel, L. (2019). Emotional Intelligence Frameworks, Charts, Diagrams & Graphs https://positivepsychology.com/emotional-intelligence-frameworks/

According to a 2016 Korn Ferry/Hay Group study, women executives are ranked highest in traits of emotional intelligence related to self-awareness, coaching/mentorship, teamwork, adaptability,

Chapter 1: **Dr. Airies Davis**

influence, and empathy. Particularly, women were ranked higher in workplace situations where they were required to lead by influence rather than directives or authority. Furthermore, the data suggests leaders who scored highest in social and emotional intelligence are organizationally effective leaders. These leaders exhibit competencies of being able to influence others, grow talent, and manage conflict. Men were equally ranked in self-control. The United States Bureau of Labor Statistics reports 109,000 more women in the workplace than men. Women maintain dominance in five core industry sectors: healthcare and social, education, non-profit, human resources, and customer service. In Q1 2020, women occupied 50.04 percent more positions than men, yet, men continue to vastly outnumber women in leadership roles. Even more surprising, women are often made to feel like outsiders upon being advanced to C-suite level leadership roles.

In order to garner a broad spectrum of the aforementioned emotional intelligence leadership competencies, I asked cisgender female leaders I respect and admire to answer a prompt to be included in this chapter. The responses were extracted from my intimate sphere of emotionally intelligent and influential women leaders. The question prompt asks the women leaders to: "Reflect on your professional experiences as a woman leader, especially compared to male counterparts. What one superhero or SHEro power is essential for women to effectively lead in the workplace? Why?"

Also, as a life-long learner and practitioner-scholar, it is important that readers are able to utilize the four emotional intelligent superpowers in practice. Bloom's Taxonomy framework of learning suggests higher-order metacognition or retention (remembering) occurs during reflection. Accordingly, readers are encouraged to take a moment to review the reflection question prompts following each emotional intelligence leadership power section.

Self-Awareness: Invisible Plane to Fly Above Imposter Syndrome

The first Wonder Woman leadership power is **self-awareness** and its relation to how you show up at work. Self-awareness is demonstrative of one's emotional state and its behavioral impact on others. As a woman leader often in male-dominated environments, are you representing your authentic self or an imposter version of your true self/identity? Often, imposter syndrome emerges in the form of self-doubt and lack of confidence in our capabilities and skills at work. A 2008 Harvard Business Review article refers to the imposter syndrome as "a collection of feelings of inadequacy that persist despite evident success." Research defines the imposter syndrome as a "psychological behavioral pattern in which one's doubts are replaced with internalized fear of exposure as a fraud or misrepresentation of actual skills." Our self-efficacy or belief in the ability to exert control over career-related decisions and behavioral motivations are occasionally lacking when compared to male counterparts.

As an emerging organizational/talent development leader entering the world of work for a Big 4 professional services firm, a job interview set the stage for an inaugural personal test of self-awareness. In preparation for an esteemed junior-level role, I checked all of the professional interview boxes; I arrived early, wore business attire, and had a folio full of cardstock resumes in tote. A quick scan of the waiting area revealed a sea of men; I was the only woman and person of color awaiting an interview. To my astonishment and with barely a glance of acknowledgment, I was instructed to have a seat and handed an administrative assistant exam. Another scan of the

Chapter 1: **Dr. Airies Davis**

room confirmed I was the only candidate asked to take the administrative assistant exam. The macroaggressions or overt discrimination of bias and the sense of being marginalized were evident. Due to imposter syndrome, I even considered that perhaps my qualifications were not up to par with my male counterparts vying for the same job. Fundamentally, I was not self-aware enough of my qualifications and talents. Many workplace scenarios do not foster environments to allow women to show up whole. Some studies refer to this as representing your 'whole person.' Effectively, women leaders are forced to only display a minute semblance of their full selves. As reflected in the aforementioned personal journey, it is imperative as women leaders to utilize our superpowers to fly above imposter syndromes and feelings of being unworthy. Fortunately, with encouragement and support from the Big 4 National Diversity Officer, I was able to land the job!

Commonly, the void of self-awareness results in women leaders feeling unworthy and not deserving of achieving heightened levels of success despite external evidence to the contrary. Wonder Woman Influencer Dr. Bonita Carr, an Executive Director of a non-profit, suggests the necessity to build upon the ultimate foundational "belief in oneself in spite of the odds, the dangers, track record, racism, or critics" to counter imposter syndrome and build self-awareness. Furthermore, millennial entrepreneur Miki Grace, Chief Experience Officer of Mining Love in the Gap, refers to the superpower of "creative confidence" as being an essential superpower especially for women of color in leadership to build self-awareness. Miki states in part:

> "Creative confidence [allows women] to believe our ideas and solutions are just as bold, brilliant, and necessary as anyone else in the room. It is important that [women leaders] demonstrate

creative confidence in the workplace...to offer meaningful solutions that inspire positive impactful change and differentiated approaches. When women leaders hold back (at work) we further deprive the world in need and ultimately, harm ourselves. I have learned instead of shrinking in the workplace and resenting myself for doing so, I must take more opportunities to practice and build my capacity for creative confidence by speaking up whenever I have a big idea."

Key indicators suggest the importance of women using self-awareness to discern moments where they may deem it important to "behave like men" in leadership at work. Exercising this method of self-awareness around belief in oneself and creative confidence can result in women leaders changing behaviors and societal transformations. Self-awareness emotions are often viewed as a leveler across genders.

REFLECTIONS of a Wonder Woman: *What practices will you implement and/or change at work so you can build or increase your self-awareness? In what ways can and/or do you show up as your authentic self to circumvent imposter syndrome?*

Self-Management: Amazonian Agility/Adaptability to Shield Adversity

Exercising sensitivity to empathize with another person's feelings while self-managing or controlling one's emotions and behaviors is the second superpower of emotionally intelligent women leaders. Amazonian Wonder Women leaders display self-management in the form of agility and adaptability, often in an attempt to shield themselves from adversity at work. Empathetic leaders with the trait of self-management are able to adequately harness emotions such as

Chapter 1: **Dr. Airies Davis**

fear, anger, and disappointment while shielding its interference with the ability to listen and problem solve. Empathy in leadership encourages cooperation and collaboration.

Take Fary Warren, Manager Strategic Billing Gas Transportation at an Illinois gas company, who noted self-management as an essential superpower in her role to effectively motivate her multigenerational team of diverse talent. Fary believes an emphatic and agile leader capable of controlling their emotions will encourage talent to not only show up for work but to perform. She created a "stand and deliver" exercise at the start of meetings to provide a safe space for her team to share and reflect on their emotional state. Fary intensely listens without judgment or opinion to offer motivating notes of encouragement. In this example, empathy can be used to understand how employees interrelate with the goal of creating authentic bonds. Also, consider city of Chicago SHEro Mayor Lori Lightfoot leading a population of over 2.6 million amidst adversity during the worldwide COVID19 pandemic. In one of her many SHEroic outcomes, Mayor Lightfoot, often considered emoting a "serious face," creatively exercised empathetic and sensitive language by using memes and social media videos to build a serious case for staying at home. In both cases, the Wonder Woman leaders interrelated self-management as a vital tool to adapt collaboration and cooperation.

Moreover, powerful leadership is an emotion-laden process whereby empathetic leaders are viewed as competent at managing their emotions resulting in being considered more effective at work. Wonder Woman Influencer Tanya Burks, U.S. Executive Search Leader at Aon Corporation, also describes this self-management capacity as "mental toughness." Tanya further states that the agility to lead by using gut intuition is a part of the mental toughness women need to endure business cycles. The use of gut intuition while in my role as Assistant Vice President for an investment and wealth management firm became even more prevalent during the 2008 financial crisis. This period of using self-management at work was instrumental in forever changing the trajectory of my mental toughness. I was charged with partnering with male C-suite level business executives to successfully lead talent transition and merger plans. To be successful in this role, it was important to self-manage emotions and trust intuitions. Recognizing mental toughness or grit to stick with the task at hand was an instrumental indicator toward enhancing my emotional intelligence superpowers. This mental toughness led to a successful joint partnership where my voice was not only heard but respected. Research has proven that managed emotions can drive trust and loyalty toward work commitments.

REFLECTIONS of a Wonder Woman: Think about a moment when you felt the need to be agile in order to adapt your behavior at work and exercise empathy towards someone else. Why/how did you self-manage your behavior?

Social Awareness: Twirl the Golden Lasso of Truth

The third superpower of emotionally intelligent women leaders is social awareness. Social awareness is one's ability to understand, respond, and sense the emotions of others and feel comfortable socially. Being socially aware affords women leaders the ability to instantaneously gather, sort, and manage emotional truths to drive bold decision-making. Wonder Woman twirls her golden lasso of truth around enemies as a method of gaining information in order to exercise justice or social awareness before making decisions.

Chapter 1: **Dr. Airies Davis**

Leadership Coach and Organizational Culture Expert Kimberly Penharlow offers bold decisiveness and clear communication as an all-inclusive collaborative approach toward building social and emotional awareness. She expounds that confident woman leaders who make and communicate decisions to develop fellowships across their organization should be celebrated. A personal example of social awareness using bold decision-making showed up during my role as a Senior Trainer driving client adoption at a leading job board. As an early adopter of digital and remote learning environments, I traveled over 75 percent nationally while interacting with multifaceted talent demographics and organizations spanning various industries. One training session for 100+ people in the male-dominated automotive industry led me to a rural farm town. I was literally the only person of color and a part of less than 10 percent of women in the audience make-up. Almost instantly upon walking into the venue, I became socially aware, sensing emotional discomfort, uncertainty, and fear from the audience. It is a skill to be able to read, uncover, and sense the true mood in a room. As any great Wonder Woman with a lasso in tote, in order to understand and respond to the emotions of the audience prior to starting the session, I engaged in personal storytelling and audience conversations. In these one-on-ones, I was able to personally relate to the audience members with my background of being born in rural Mississippi. As I began my introduction at the start of the session, instead of the archetypal scripted background overview, I told human-centered stories from those early individual audience discussions. This allowed a sense of relatable emotional connection and social comfort from the audience. Equally, I felt empowered to deliver the content as a respected and trustworthy subject-matter expert and conduit of knowledge.

Social awareness at work affords women leaders the emotional intelligence to respond as active listeners. Active listening refers to the art of listening to others in order to gather what is really being said or deemed truthful. As a Senior Strategist providing human-centered consultation, clients seek my expertise as a critical thinker with an instinct to actively listen for understanding and a unique penchant of relating to diverse audiences. One example occurred when I partnered with a talent accelerator business to convene stakeholders toward developing a think tank innovation lab to solve the problem of building a diverse talent acquisition pipeline for hard-to-fill requisitions. I had to actively listen for the truth behind the problem. This exercise of social awareness allowed me the ability to boldly respond to the range of emotional reactions from the stakeholders based on our proposed scalable solutions.

Felischa Marye, TV and Feature Film Writer of Felicity Films and Creator/Showrunner of BIGGER on BET Networks, notes active listening as a form of nurturing with compassion. She states the skill of active listening is what makes women unique over their male counterparts. Social awareness in the form of active listening allows women leaders to care what others are going through. Juliette Buford, Senior Director of Finance at a public broadcast station, believes many women are taught to shun the natural keen ability to own success and demonstrate care or empathetic leadership at work. Instead, women are encouraged to pursue what many would inaccurately classify as 'aggressive masculine' traits. Juliette states in part:

> "As if (being masculinity aggressive) is the only way to be powerful (at work). I have learned the power of being empathic and (caring). This has allowed me to be a "human" leader. People respond to honesty and to (women leaders) that are genuinely

Chapter 1: **Dr. Airies Davis**

interested in moving forward the mission and talent within work environments."

Leadership strength is not exclusive to men or women. Bold, decisive, empathetic nurturing, and human-centered social awareness spans across genders.

REFLECTIONS of a Wonder Woman: Describe a work-based scenario where you practiced understanding and active listening in order to neutralize a stressful situation. How did you make bold decisions while sensing emotions in order to make others comfortable?

Relationship Management: Deflect Saboteurs with Magical Silver Bracelets

Relationship management is the final superpower essential for women leaders at work. Relationship management is caring what others experience while exhibiting the ability to influence, connect, and inspire others toward managing relationships and conflict. Even though my name is Airies, I, too, face inner saboteur battles with the mythical God of war Ares, my phonetic namesake. Comparable to Wonder Woman using her magic bracelets (inner strength) to protect against nemesis' like Ares, the creation of a tribe is essential for women leaders in order to deflect saboteurs at work.

An inner saboteur attacks your self-efficacy and says that you are not powerful or important enough to exist in the boardroom or as entrepreneurs to manage relationships with male counterparts. This superpower blocks any esteem attacks to inspire us to believe and show up in our true essence. Women leaders competent to build and manage relationships are often able to transform, motivate, and create positive emotional reactions. Shannon Stone-Winding, President and

CEO of Black Alliance of Colleges and Employers (BACE), refers to this skill as "building your tribe," saying it is essential to filling relationship gaps. Shannon states in part:

> "In business, they say it is all about whom you know. However, this implies a responsibility of the knowers. Building your allies and tribe of authentic and credible folks is a necessity. Additionally, recognition of this responsibility is a...privilege. The privilege must be balanced with providing air cover and safety for the next generation of SHEro's."

The tribe can consist of institutional agents, mentors, role models, coaches, and advisors - all distinctly different resources to support women leaders in building transformational relationships. Equally, it is significant to seek a broad spectrum of tribe influencers based on gender, race, and orientation. I often call upon members of my tribe during wide-ranging facets of my professional journey for guidance.

Upon solidifying your relationships by building a tribe, it is essential to find your voice of confidence. Some researchers believe women tend to follow an emergent path to leadership at work while men tend to follow more linear or strategic paths to leadership. The intrinsic motivation to assert strength and confidence is a driving factor behind each of the gender-laced leadership paths. Dr. Rosalind Conerly, Stanford University Associate Dean and Director of Centers for Equity, Community, and Leadership found her leadership path and describes an unassuming way to exert strength and assertiveness as consistent superpowers driving her career. Moreover, she explains the ability to self-care is necessary for women leaders to heal:

Chapter 1: **Dr. Airies Davis**

"The superhero power to heal and restore myself both mentally and physically. Taking the time for me to recognize that I may be struggling in certain areas of my personal and professional life and giving myself time to recover allows me to start fresh without any guilt! This also includes giving myself affirmations and pep talks when self-doubt or disappointment starts to set in. This allows me to be a more confident, approachable, and empathetic leader because it reminds me to humanize people in the workplace."

The absence of psychological safety can prevent your ability to find your voice in order to humanize people and build relationships. Dr. Timothy Clark refers to psychological safety as feeling included, safe to learn, safe to contribute, and safe to challenge the status quo. Essentially, not all workplace environments invoke heightened levels of confidence or psychological safety for women leaders to foster, manage, and build relationships. I employ women leaders to counter this feeling with mindfulness practices in order to restore confidence.

REFLECTIONS of a Wonder Woman: *Armed with an invisible plane, a lasso, magical bracelets, and a shield, how will you use your emotional intelligence as protection against inner saboteurs? Describe your current/future work tribe. How will you employ the tribe's support during your professional journey?*

Conclusion

Our leadership SHEro powers are emotional intelligence drivers of self-awareness, self-management, social awareness, and relationship management. Wonder Women thought leaders have emerged as preeminent forces in business while continuing to battle Ares against such perils as the pay equity gap, racial and cultural injustices, and a lack of fair promotions. Yet, we continue to make our mark in the business world. To continuously create a baseline understanding of your emotional state at work, begin by creating an action list of roses (wins), thorns (challenges), and bushes (new growth ideas) you will intake as a result of what you uncovered about your leadership traits. Now that you recognize your innate powers as a Wonder Woman at work, what is your superpower and how will you continue to harness it?

CHAPTER 2

EMPATHY - THE FOUNDATION OF EQ

By **BANU RAGHURAMAN**

Intelligence is a myriad of things, not just a measure of the traditional mental aptitude. Now, an intrinsic addition is emotional intelligence (EQ) - assessing whether you can understand and react to something which cannot be seen, only felt. I believe empathy builds emotional intelligence naturally.

Can you teach empathy? Whether it be Mr. Data or Mr. Spock from *Star Trek* or Sheldon Cooper from *The Big Bang Theory*, individuals without empathy have struggled to understand other humans, who seem to feel. Yet, we are struggling as a human society to develop and find people with emotional intelligence.

Myths About Empathy

We look for people with EQ and those who see us more than a number, a resource, or an employee ID. But when we actually come across them, we have many hesitations and stereotypes instead of appreciating them.

I am one of those who cry when I watch emotional movies. All through my growing up years, I was extremely ashamed of it, as people stared or laughed at me. I always wished my eyes could somehow absorb the tears and make them disappear. Now, well into my adulthood, I still bravely tear up, but the difference is that I have accepted this as part of my nature. In recent times, when I witnessed someone being reprimanded at work or someone struggling to complete their task, I chip in. Sometimes, it meant I worked overtime, but I created a trusting relationship with someone who felt grateful toward me. I have shed tears with a colleague who lost her father and I have hugged an office cleaner who was scared to have her spinal surgery. This is the simplest expression of empathy - when you see another in pain, you feel their pain. Yet, this ability is seen as a weakness. Feeling for another is often seen as an inability to be strong. Worse still as a woman, I was labeled as being emotional or "soft."

I have even been passed over for a promotion. Even though my performance reflected excellence, the approach I took was empathetic. It took a little longer, perhaps, ensuring everyone felt included and consulted, but the goals were achieved. And yet, my lack of aggression was seen as a negative. At the time, my manager felt that I wasn't capable of leading a team because I came across as "soft." The time investment to work toward a solution that empathized with all stakeholders was at a cost they did not favor and that worked against me. Even though the delivery was delayed by two weeks, the outcome reflected one of the most successful projects, due to widespread acceptance of the goals by all the stakeholders. So, in spite of proven outcomes, the path I took was seen as a lack of capability. Needless to say, I was in another role by the time the manager realized the impact of the empathy I displayed.

Another myth is that empathy and assertiveness cannot exist together. And in a parallel myth, aggression is seen as assertiveness. In conflict resolution, a person who is assertive is able to achieve what they want and "win" the argument. But assertiveness is not the quality of "winning" an argument. Assertiveness is the ability to take a stand for something that matters. That something is fully weighed in pros and cons and seen as the best decision within the related constraints for the required outcome. In a true sense, assertiveness cannot be achieved without empathy, because you need to assess the best choice in as many aspects as possible, and stand behind the decision for the right reasons. If new information comes to light, assertiveness should not be enforced for the wrong reasons.

Aggression, in fact, can only result in a more delicate situation, especially in the long term. While being in a role that required negotiation, my manager asked another gentleman in my team to step in, as he thought I would need "support" during the negotiation. During the conversation, the "support" person dominated the discussion, while I stayed on the call as a resource that confirmed administrative details. Not only did the opposite party find it fishy that someone had just taken over the business relationship, but they also found his aggressive attitude complacent and disrespectful. As you may have guessed, they wished to withdraw from the conversation and then escalated the unhappy situation.

These are only a few of many myths about empathy. It is not seen as an important quality and is often seen as something to be ignored, especially if you have any hope of achieving personal gains or goals. Empathy is not seen as part of personality building. Empathy is not seen as a winning quality. Empathy is not seen as something that helps a person progress.

Why Is Empathy Important in Leadership?

Leadership and success are no longer just dependent on Intelligence Quotient (IQ). Leaders are assessed on their ability to 'deeply move' their followers. Some of the world's best leaders, from Mahatma Gandhi to Barack Obama to Jacinda Ardern - every one of them has understood the importance of inspiring from the heart. Understanding what drives people to give their best and feel passionate about the brand and their work is now even more important than the technical skills of a leader. The world has definitely shifted from the focus of technical skills, as those can be acquired by learning in a teaching environment. But what cannot be learnt is the innate ability to feel for another.

When hiring in the IT domain, technical skills are crucial for the roles. But the few months of a probationary period is an important time for me to observe how well the new hire gels with the rest of the team. This is the time when they are most vulnerable, being the newest member of our little zoo. How they protect themselves or another team member, what excuses they come up with, how they represent their team - all of these become indicators and a foundation of how their relationship and performance will progress. If at this stage they can work with empathy, then their attitude during the best of times will be even better. To some extent, training programs can ramp up the employee's technical skills if they are lacking. This is a smaller cost to how much you may lose by having a distressing team member who brings the team morale down or is difficult to work with.

As a woman, I have to touch on the nurturer versus provider[1] debate, which easily tilts in favour of being a woman. Many corporate programs are being developed to bring women into leadership roles. Revolutions around diversity, inclusion, and gender balance are improving the awareness around these issues in various societies. But as a biological nurturer, most women are naturally built for the role of a leader. If we define years of practice as an indication of skill, then think about all the women, who as little girls were taught to take care of a doll or a baby. They were the first to learn to think of someone apart from themselves. To add on some marital humor, she takes up the role of running a household with no prior knowledge and she runs it successfully like clockwork, navigating family dynamics, in-laws' expectations, and handling all of the wife-targeted humor, with the ease of a seasoned politician.

I want to add an important point here that while I wholeheartedly support the diversity and inclusion of women in leadership roles, I am against and discourage the promotion of female leaders just for the sake of it. Shaping potential female leaders into stronger leaders is a very different approach compared to deliberately promoting them into roles they are not yet ready to take on. This will only cause unhappiness in the team, encourage rumors of favoritism, or sow disbelief in the program itself.

Unfortunately, there are still old-school thinkers who box women into specific roles. On the other hand, women themselves do not see enough representation in certain roles or industries to think of themselves as capable. In fact, there are studies that say the upbringing of a female child is radically different than that of a male child, which intrinsically affects their ability to be a leader[2]. The empathy that the female child is innately born with is deflected into pleasing everyone, instead of using it as a capability to build herself as a strong proponent for betterment.

It is common knowledge that educating females is one of the best ways to improve the state of families in developing countries[3]. And before someone thinks this is a sexist sentiment - it simply stems from the fact that in these developing nations, women are still the ones taking care of children. While educated males are able to earn better at the workplace, they are not able to invest in the mental growth and development of the next generation. It is the female caretakers who spend most of the time with their kids - and hence, it makes sense that women be educated well so that they instill the joy of education in their kids and build on the capability of future leaders. So, if the leaders are just a group of men, they probably will never realize why women need to be educated in these circumstances. Think about how the impacts would radically change if a female leader was present at these decision-making conversations. A classic example is an incident where a group of male political leaders made decisions on laws around abortion[4].

More important than the other two aspects discussed earlier, let's see where business, techniques, and toolkits are heading - what does the customer want? And for businesses to truly survive - what does the customer need? Without truly putting yourself in the shoes of your customer, how will you determine what they want or need? Yes, surveys, focus groups, and other data collection techniques are common ways of assessing what people want. But beyond that, we need to humanize the information to make sure the details have innate empathy of what the customers and consumers are feeling.

Let's look at how Gilette captured the female razor market[5]. Prior to Gilette's ingenious idea, there was no market for females wanting to remove body hair. It was absolutely natural to be natural. Yet, by understanding the female need to be physically attractive and good looking, they extended their ads to create a new need that is still going strong today. The negative ethical, body image, and self-confidence impacts this ad campaign created is a debate for another day, but consider the breakthrough this business made by simply thinking about the feelings of the potential customers, rather than just removing body hair of the customer. Empathy - the ability to put yourself in another's shoes - brings in a whole new perspective you can only tap into if you choose to allow yourself to feel.

So, there is no doubt that by looking at the empathy dimension, businesses and leaders can push the boundaries of what was possible. And these possibilities can transcend multiple generations and revolutionize new cultural expectations.

How Do You Develop Empathy As a Leader?

The best way of knowing what another person is going through is by putting yourself in their shoes. Unless it is "Freaky Friday," that may not be completely possible, but you can definitely volunteer to try their work hands-on. Often, managers in companies are individuals who have experienced the hands-on work that they eventually learn to manage with other resources. When you move into a leadership position, without insight into what happens at the grass-root level, you lose the connection with the employee, as you do not appreciate the challenges of their role. And if you do not understand, how will you facilitate or resolve their issues? By working hands-on, even temporarily, you gain that empathy in the workplace. Of course, you can again resort to informational interviews, coffee conversations, or peer review feedback, but nothing will give you the same level of insight as doing it yourself. The work is not just the mechanical execution of the task itself, but it is the elation and frustration that can only be experienced hands-on, especially for someone who is learning empathy.

Every company has its own culture, but there are always unconscious subcultures that form due to managerial or departmental leader influences. One of the key aspects these subcultures vary in is the feeling of security among employees. Fear makes us do strange and vile things and often culminates in destructive behaviors. And eventually, it is little surprise that the destructive feelings will affect your bottom line and the morale of your team.

How often have you been in an initiative where you are reinventing the wheel or spending time uncovering what an existing system does, just because the current process owner refuses to divulge the details? Even after hours of asking questions, coffee dates, and placating, you cannot break through their steel exterior. No surprise that this is going to impact project costs. Had the same approach been taken with clear communication of project goals, an openness to continue providing job security in the new world, and using empathy to make decisions in this emotional time can definitely lead to better results.

It is important to note that as a business, you cannot always guarantee that employees' jobs are secure at all times, but being cognizant of how the changes and communication will impact employees and being transparent and supportive toward them can definitely turn a situation toward something better.

As a leader, it is important to ensure everyone on your team is open to sharing information. Showing genuine concern and helping each other should not be punitive, but encouraged. By sharing, we are caring. And by caring, empathy builds up within a team. Looking out for one another within a team setting is the first step to building a highly functional team[6]. Caring is the first step to building trustworthy communication channels. Even though this may start as a "status update" style to "impress the boss," assimilating communication into the culture will encourage the importance of sharing details to help each other. And as with all other aspects of change management, the action should start from you as the leader. Show kindness to your employees and reap the benefits of loyalty and a secure team driven to give their best.

A common bias that women leaders are affected by is that they are always measured by their level of likeability[7]. It is a tough boat to balance. However, as with all other situations, genuine expressions bring the best results. As a leader, you have access to a view that everyone else on your team lacks - combine that information with empathy to reap the best results. Good leaders are not made overnight because of one action. They go through multiple ups and downs, and they emerge strong at the end. What is important to note is that female leadership is not meant to replace male leadership. Both aspects - the yin and the yang - have to coexist for a successful venture.

A generic thought when working toward building empathy: Embark with an open mind, as you would when building any other new team skill. Preconceived notions and biases can affect the quality of the outcomes[8]. Regular feedback and review of the mental health of the team is a good quality metric. While empathy cannot be directly measured, it manifests itself in different actions toward the growth of your team. Similarly, it is not a "one solution fits all" situation. Use empathy to identify what your team needs and balance that with the business' needs.

I want to sign off by saying that, in the midst of competition, profitability, and all of the other tangible benefits a leader needs to keep track of, empathy adds a dimension of intelligence and humanity important in a world riddled with issues of divisiveness and ego.

"In a world where you can be anything, be kind."
–Jennifer Dukes Lee

Disclaimer: The opinions shared in this article are based on the author's experiences and are provided for illustrative purposes.

---

[1] https://www.psychologytoday.com/ca/blog/the-caregivers-handbook/201204/man-the-fixer-woman-the-nurturer-the-caregiving-gender-gap

[2] https://www.ted.com/talks/reshma_saujani_teach_girls_bravery_not_perfection?language=en

[3] https://www.globalpartnership.org/blog/why-educating-girls-makes-economic-sense

[4] https://www.usatoday.com/story/news/nation/2019/05/15/alabama-abortion-law-american-views-abortion-poll-pro-life-pro-choice-republicans-catholic-heartbeat/3678315002/

[5] https://www.bustle.com/articles/196747-the-sneaky-manipulative-history-of-why-women-started-shaving

[6] https://www.youtube.com/watch?v=YPDmNaEG8v4

[7] https://www.forbes.com/sites/pragyaagarwaleurope/2018/10/23/not-very-likeable-here-is-how-bias-is-affecting-women-leaders/#b7cf50f295fd

[8] https://www.earth.com/news/preconceived-notions-emotions/

CHAPTER 3

FAILING INTO SUCCESS

By **CAMILLA JEFFS**

As business owners, as parents, and as people, it is natural to hide your failures and celebrate your successes. You want to shout your triumphs from the rooftop and bury the failures out in the backyard.

For many people, this is normal. I felt that way, too. I was raised to be a housewife and not a CEO. I didn't have business modeled to me and I didn't learn financial responsibility or resilience in school.

Now, as a successful entrepreneur and mother, I strive to be completely transparent with my kids about failure, resilience, accountability, work habits, and responsibility. I teach them about passion and how to take control of their lives regardless of other people's expectations.

Most of all, I teach my children what it means to fail at something, to be bad at something and learn from it, and how failures make you a better person, a better parent, and a better entrepreneur.

One recent example comes to mind. As part of my real estate business, I had to learn online marketing. To stretch myself and try to become more effective, I often learn new software and methods to grow my business. Recently, I started learning an online mailing service and sent out my first official business newsletter.

Not knowing any better, I took my thousands of contacts and dumped them into the mailing service system. When that first newsletter hit their inboxes, hundreds of people unsubscribed and cited it as spam. I was mortified. I didn't want to be a "spammer." To add insult to injury, the mailing service thought I was misusing their service and blocked my account.

My first newsletter failed spectacularly.

I learned from the experience, posted the required opt-in form for people to sign up, reworked my newsletter, and sent out my second one to a mere 82 people. I felt so small.

After a day of wallowing, I decided to use this incident as an opportunity to speak to my kids. I wanted to show them that failure comes in many forms. Failing doesn't only mean the big things like failing a class, losing a business, or missing out on a lot of money. Failure can be any size and to me, my newsletter debacle was a failure. It would have been easy to just stop and not send out newsletters at all. After all, I wasn't good at it, right?

But instead, I showed my teenage kids the software and explained what happened, how I had messed up, and what steps I was taking to make sure that wouldn't happen again. I explained what lessons I learned from the situation and discussed how I can apply those lessons to other parts of my business.

Chapter 3: **Camilla Jeffs**

I want my kids to see that adults fail, too. Parents are not perfect; we don't know all the answers. And I need to model the right behavior for how to react to failure, pick yourself back up, learn from it, and move forward with a better understanding of what to do - and what not to do - next time.

There are six main lessons I want to teach my children and other entrepreneurs. Those are: failing with grace, working hard, working smart, asking for help, financial responsibility, and choosing your own path.

Failing With Grace

As a child, I suffered from perfectionism. Failure was simply not an option, and because I didn't fail, I only attempted challenges I knew I could succeed at. I wanted to be perfect all the time and I had to do everything myself so it was done right. The need for perfection and the internal pressure continued on into adulthood. I didn't think anything was wrong with this mentality - after all, we all want things to be perfect, to be done well, to be right.

Then I started noticing that perfectionism in my children. They were putting that intense pressure on themselves, too, giving up easily, and getting angry when things didn't go the way they thought it should. When you notice your own negative traits in your kids, you see how damaging and difficult they can be. It inspired me to look inside myself and try to make a change. The kids were just doing what they had always seen me do, and it was not good for them. Which meant it probably wasn't good for me, either.

I started doing research and read a lot of books. One in particular that helped was Mindset by Carol Dweck, Ph.D. I learned about fixed mindset versus growth mindset and how having a growth mindset means you can expand, learn new things, and grow. You will be bad at first and then get better with practice. Think about a child who is learning to take their first steps. No adult will scold or be angry if they fall. And no child gives up learning to walk. A fixed mindset tells you that you only have your natural abilities and that is it. There is no growth or change. I started growing and retraining my mindset and myself.

In high school, I was an athlete. I was a sprinter on the school track team and had somehow gotten it in my head that I was only good at sprinting. I couldn't do distance running, I just didn't have the stamina or endurance for long races. I truly believed my muscles were only good at fast things, like sprinting. After my fifth child turned one, I wanted to stretch my new growth mindset. I decided to train for a half IRONMAN triathlon. The half IRONMAN triathlon is a 1.2-mile swim, 56-mile bike ride, and a 13.1-mile run. I set a big goal for myself and trained for an entire year. There were times I wanted to stop, there was pain, there was failure in the training process.

There was a moment during the race where I didn't think I could finish. The swim went relatively well, but the bike was grueling. As I came into the transition from bike to run, I had already been exercising for four straight hours. As I sat on the ground changing my shoes, my body was screaming at me to stop. Every muscle ached, I was sunburnt badly because my bike shorts rode up too high, and I was spent. I hung my head, seriously contemplating ending the journey there. No one would have been upset with me except myself. So, I dug deep. It took every ounce of willpower to pull that body off the ground, stumble to the volunteer lathering people with more sunscreen, and then force myself to begin a two-hour run. I plastered a smile on my face as I high-fived my little children eagerly waiting to cheer for Mommy.

It wasn't pretty, but I did it! I accomplished my goal and completed the half IRONMAN triathlon. I have the pictures of me adorned with a medal smiling with my children, and I also have the reality picture of me hanging my head in utter exhaustion. And I will forever be grateful. That experience alone has pushed me through the majority of my darkest moments, my failures, and times I wanted to quit. Training for a half IRONMAN was a long process and difficult to learn to admit my failures, not only to myself but out loud to others. But it has been an important step in my life.

Ultimately, I want my kids to learn that failure is a part of the learning process. It is expected and it WILL happen. It's never a matter of if, just a matter of when. When kids see their parents fail and get back up, take responsibility, and do better next time, they learn a powerful lesson about life and business.

Working Hard

Part of success in business and in life is working hard. My husband and I work very hard evaluating and purchasing properties, managing them, and rehabbing homes in our real estate business. To have a successful business, you need dedication and a willingness to work hard.

Hard work is not only rewarding, but it can also be fun. Sometimes it takes a child to point out the fun moments. When the kids were little, my husband and I owned a fourplex and we couldn't find help to clear the parking lot in the winter. We'd had a storm and there was a six-inch layer of ice in the parking lot that was a danger to the residents.

There was no one else to do the work, so we packed up all the kids and went out to the parking lot with hammers, poles, and sticks and busted up ice for several hours. There were many moments I wanted to quit or thought it was too hard or too much for the kids. But as I was over there sweating and worrying, the kids would look up and grin and tell me this was the best day ever!

Working Smart

As entrepreneurs, we often feel the need to do everything ourselves when we start a business. When I started mine, I did everything. I had to, out of necessity. I didn't have anyone to help and I wanted my business to succeed.

You can only go so far if you insist on doing everything yourself. While it was very valuable and I learned a lot from the experience, I had to start working smarter and automating or outsourcing certain things so the business could grow and so my expertise could go to more important pieces of the business.

I like involving my kids in my business, so when I need to outsource things, I present them to my teenagers first. I let them know what I need to hire someone for and ask if there is anything on the list that they are interested in learning. My 15-year-old had been wanting to learn more about video editing and I recently hired her to edit videos for my business. She has learned iMovie and QuickTime and has been doing more research and learning on her own. Her twin sister dove into website design and is learning how to code in WordPress.

My 17-year-old does all my graphic design. My 12-year-old helps set up the video equipment for webinars and videos. And my 9-year-old, well, she makes us laugh. The kids are not only helping the business, but also learning new skills and earning money. Win-win!

Asking for Help

Similar to working smart and learning when to outsource or automate, business owners also need to be able to ask for help when they need it. You can't stretch yourself so thin that you can't get anything done. Not just in business, but also in life.

For example, an injury can sideline you but work still needs to get done and if you try to do it yourself, you may hurt yourself more and still not get the project done. Once, during a home renovation, I hurt my neck. I couldn't carry heavy things or do physical labor and we typically didn't ask the kids to do the heavy lifting. At first, I just kept doing it anyway but the pain got worse and I had to accept I couldn't do it.

I asked the older kids for help. They were already involved in a lot of smaller projects, but I needed them for the bigger things, too. I worried about them getting hurt or saying no, but interestingly, the moment I allowed them to help with bigger things, the more they wanted to do.

Again, I had to let go of perfection and allow the kids to learn. And they ended up learning so much faster than if I hadn't been hurt and trying to micromanage. Asking for help and being willing to pitch in when needed is important in every aspect of life!

Financial Preparedness

The American education system does not teach fiscal responsibility, and that is hurting us as a society. Many young adults are not really financially prepared or know what to do to be fiscally responsible. They will say, "Oh, I heard I need a 401(k). I don't know what it is, but I got one."

We have instituted some things in our family to teach our kids about money. They have their regular chores they're required to do and then a bunch of extra chores they can do to earn money whenever they want. Any money they get, they have to donate 10% and save 10%. In addition, we have a "family bank," where the more they save, the more we pay.

We also speak very openly about finances and money. Whenever we are thinking about buying an investment property, we sit down with the kids and talk about it. We explain where the money comes from, what it's buying, how to analyze investment properties, how to manage tenants, what rent is, and more.

We teach them about consumer debt and why we avoid it. If they ask for big things, like a boat, we explain why we will not go into debt to buy one. We are adamant that they not take student loans for college if at all possible. We want our kids to understand money and fiscal responsibility and know they have options.

For example, we do not tell our kids that college is a requirement. If they want to go to college, great. My oldest daughter wants to, and we've recently set her up with apps and research to start looking for and applying for scholarships. We've also been teaching the older kids ways they may be able to pay for school through real estate, such as owning a fourplex and living in one unit and renting out the rest. We are also teaching them about entrepreneurship and online businesses and what it means to diversify income streams.

Choosing Your Path

As I said, we aren't telling our kids they have to go to college and get a degree to be successful. I want them to find their passion and pursue it even if it doesn't come from college. I went to college and got a bachelor's degree in English education with the intent to be a teacher before deciding not to go that route.

I was raised to be a stay at home mother and support my husband. While I do not believe that is all I am anymore, I want my kids to know they can be a spouse plus so much more. At 37 years old, after I'd had all of my kids, I went back to school to get an MBA. I commuted five hours per day to go to the program and it was intense. It was hard for me and the kids and my husband. But I showed them that they can pursue a passion even if they have a family. All of my kids made posters and cheered for me at graduation.

Now they know they can dream big, find the things they love, and doggedly pursue them.

As a female entrepreneur, I believe it is important to be transparent with my kids about both my failures and successes. I want my kids to learn resilience, accountability, and responsibility. I need them to see my failures so they have realistic views of life and not expect perfection from everything on the first try. Adults - parents - are certainly not perfect. Part of preparing children for life is showing them real issues and modeling how to pick yourself back up after a fall is crucial.

Some of the most important lessons I will ever teach my kids are failing with grace, how to work hard and smart, knowing they don't have to do everything alone, financial responsibility, and to choose their own path regardless of outside expectations.

CHAPTER 4

AUTHORITY MARKETING 101

By **CAROLYN BARTH, CEO, DIGITAL CONTENT STRATEGY LLC**

I've done Authority Marketing, Public Relations, and Media across channels since the mid-90s. While writing original websites for brands like Suave Shampoo, its featured influencer was Elisabeth from the reality show Survivor. Meanwhile, a Unilever female executive launched its lucrative Dove Real Beauty campaign and became the industry authority.

Twenty years later, changes and challenges still remain for women in business. Gen Z college students are realizing the hardships: a gender pay gap, few women on corporate boards and CEO roles. My 18-year-old asks, "How do you become an industry authority known for your expertise in an era of influencers? How can women become CEOs and position themselves to be recruited for corporate boards so that their authority permits action?"

My advice is to begin with authority marketing and social proof.

Why do women in business need "social proof" today?

Close your eyes.

Think of your key competitor. The one who is known as the "best" in your industry. The one who has a waiting list of clients willing to pay top dollar for their time and knowledge gets plum speaking opportunities, and invitations to join corporate boards of directors.

Keep your eyes closed.

What would your day look like if you were widely regarded as the "go-to" industry expert? Your bio shows that you are an award-winning expert, regularly featured in the news as the industry authority on this issue, who receives respect from peers as well as the public.

Now ask yourself this: what are you waiting for? Open your eyes, and consider if authority marketing can position you as the best in your field.

3 Tips For Authority Marketing

In the past decade, I have trained more than 500 industry executives on how to do authority marketing in order to serve as spokespersons, key opinion leaders, and thought leaders for their profession. Jargon in marketing is everywhere and terms change, so at the basic level, authority marketing acts to change public and peer perception of you as an expert.

It used to be that corporate communications had three levers to pull to drive sales:

1. **Marketing is used to sell something.**
2. **Advertising is used to reinforce commonly held beliefs about a brand or person.**

3. **Public relations can establish the reputation of a person or brand, or is used to change perception with the public or peers (visibility, brand awareness, authority marketing).**

In the past six months, emotional marketing, authority marketing, and reputation management are terms that have become more widely used. Regarding advertising, you'll hear paid search and paid social used now as key terms.

This chapter is focused on authority marketing, which is a new term for many proven public relations strategies to make a message stick, build and establish a reputation, and back it up with "social proof." Social proof is things like online reviews and testimonials; publications that present you as a thought leader; having a large following on social media channels of influence; media interviews and features of your expertise; speaking opportunities; and more. Writing a chapter for this book, *Women in Business*, is a great example of the right way to begin doing authority marketing. Writing and marketing your own book and brand (personal and professional) is even stronger social proof.

Between you and me, if you are reading this book, you are probably already an expert in your field. You are operating in your genius zone, yet you may be the best-kept secret in your industry.

It's likely that your competition is better at implementing authority marketing tactics (getting interviewed in the news, collecting reviews, testimonials, and case studies, publishing articles, columns, and books, and speaking). They've mastered communicating not one-to-one, but rather one-to-many. Luckily, that's my specialty.

Have no fear! Authority marketing is a disciplined practice and strategy. Authority marketing of you as a thought leader is attainable. As long as you have industry expertise, you don't need a fancy PR or authority marketing firm to get started. A few controlled media placements in prominent publications with high domain authority (80+) to drive SEO, a monthly CEO column, or a book chapter is golden. The goal is to educate others using your authentic expertise in order to demonstrate your knowledge and command of nuanced issues facing your industry.

5 Insights into Authority Marketing from a PR Professional

1. Communicate Complex Information in Simple Language

When you can communicate complex issues facing your industry in easier-to-understand terms, you demonstrate that you understand your topic well enough to teach it. Avoid jargon and use simple language as even PhDs prefer it for an article, speech, or podcast.

2. Google Never Forgets

If you don't yet have a digital reputation, build it. When peers tell you that you are the only one who can answer a specific question, take note. Your knowledge shouldn't remain in a one-to-one conversation and if featured in the news, could go one-to-many.

Caution: Be careful about what your first story is and make sure it conveys your expertise. Develop your talking points. Focus on three things you want the world (or your industry peers) to know. Are they scientifically accurate? Do they add value to the conversation? Could you develop a compelling keynote speech on this topic on a deeper level if you had zero time to prepare? As you establish your reputation, *you'll become a trusted source as perceived by your peers. It's far easier to do proactive PR and authority building right the first time. It's much harder to fix a damaged reputation. That requires a reactive PR strategy, also known as crisis management. It's more fun and far less expensive to prevent a crisis than to fix one - and Google never forgets.*

3. **Checklist: Key Elements of Authority Marketing**
    Ensure that you have and display the following:
    a. Social Proof
        i.   Testimonials
        ii. Online Reviews
        iii. Awards
        iv. Articles/Publications You Wrote
        v.   Being Featured In the News
        vi. Speaking Opportunities
        vii. Prominent Positions (Boards of directors roles)
        viii. Social Media Smarts (The right messaging, the right channels, the right format for each channel to position you as an authority, etc.)
    b. Your Why of Your Story with Three Bullet Points and One Call to Action
    c. Your Elevator Pitch or Seven-Second Intro of Your Personal & Professional Brand

4. **How Do You Get More Authority?**
    One way to get more authority is to write a chapter in an industry-related book or write your own book that benefits your industry and adds value to it. To think about the topic of your chapter or book, reflect on what questions no one is asking in your industry yet which

need to be asked. Think about what everyone is already asking, yet is not currently being adequately answered. The answer to those two queries will identify areas where you can position yourself as an authority and add direct value to your industry.

5. What Happens Once You've Gotten Authority?

Once you've done the steps and been featured, gotten reviews, and become known as an authority in your field, you'll find that your new reputation sticks. Peers will come to you as the expert to ask questions; friends and family will understand your work more; you'll begin to create a community around you; new opportunities will present themselves; you may find that you receive more awards; and you'll see a huge uptick in referrals for new clients.

As your authority and expertise build, it's time to nurture that in a grassroots sales strategy. Clients want to work with the best and will pay top dollar to do so, so by building your authority and reputation, you are positioning yourself as the best. Continue to create great content, answer questions, and solve pain points in the industry. Make sure you empower the champions and heroes of your new 24/7 grassroots sales team, namely employees and colleagues, friends and family, other industry leaders, people who need mentorship, your community, and your key stakeholders. Empower them by giving them something to share with others about your accomplishments or features. Reward them for referrals.

Finally, protect your reputation and make sure to remain an industry authority. Google yourself monthly so you can monitor what is being said about you. If you don't like what you see, publish more social proof. Be careful about what you're posting on social media and other digital channels. Ask others how your posts and content sound and comes across. Don't preach - teach; you want to offer insight and be kind to followers. If you are new to doing media, opt for guaranteed, controlled features that proactively position you as an authority and guarantee respect. Choose your first earned media opportunities wisely.

So, let's return to the exercise from the beginning of this chapter.

Close your eyes. Imagine your competition. Consider what they are doing to position themselves in your industry as the top authority. What kind of social proof do they have for their personal and professional brand? Make a mental note so that you can do the same.

Let's learn from their success.

Now, imagine your future self as an authority in your industry. What will your day be like when clients actively seek you out to work with you and want to pay top dollar for your expertise? Who will be your champions and heroes on your future 24/7 grassroots sales team? Who is an industry leader that you can get to know better and collaborate with as your authority builds? Who will review your work and ensure accuracy, insight, and that it stays on brand?

Most importantly, before you open your eyes, what do you want to be known for? What's your legacy as a leader in your field? What do you do or know better than anyone else? This is your genius zone.

Take a deep breath. Open your eyes. Get started today. If you'd like my checklist of 29 Habits of the "Go-To" Expert, please text "29 Habits" to 312-481-6777, and I'll share it with you.

CHAPTER 5

READY TO SHINE

By **CLAUDIA ROMO EDELMAN**

As we look into the 2020s, this next decade will be about us Hispanics. I'm not saying this only as a proud Latina, but because I know it will happen. Hispanics are the new mainstream economy, the fastest-growing cohort, and the most profitable group in the country. But we have issues and gaps and we need partners to help us push the needle from recovery to shining.

I say this with confidence, as throughout my career at global institutions like the United Nations, UNICEF, the Global Fund, and the World Economic Forum, I've seen communities come out of nothing with half of what Hispanics have. Particularly now after COVID-19, and with how the social injustice conversations have shaped minds and opened hearts, there is a window of opportunity for Latinos. We must grab it.

This year, Hispanic Heritage Month was a time when people focused on our stories, voices, and data. But it cannot end with this honorary month. We must be ready, equipped, and sing from the same song sheet. We must be a united front. We must educate ourselves to be able to enlighten others. We must be proud to be able to be loud.

The official theme for the 2020 Hispanic Heritage Month was **"a history of serving our nation."** This is crucial because we have always been here. We have a history and a vast heritage to be proud of, as we have contributed to this country since the 16th century in sports, agriculture, retail, media, entertainment, and so much more. But where are these contributions listed or honored?

The U.S. as we know it would not exist without Hispanics. The Hispanic contribution is fundamental to our country and must be in our history books. Can you imagine if we were put back into history? Imagine how America would see us. More importantly, how would we see ourselves?

Even today, up until two years ago, the most-followed people on social media were Hispanic: Selena Gomez on Instagram and Shakira on Facebook. The song that broke all records and became the most streamed was "Despacito." Our cultural relevance is creating a revolution. Latin and Hispanic culture is incorporated into every area of society, touching all of our senses.

That is what I am talking about! Our time is now. And it's not just our history - we're here today. The fastest-growing, the most profitable.

We are the people of America - 60 million people comprising 18.1% of the current population. We are the future of America. By 2050, one-quarter of the population will be Hispanic.

We are the economic power. Hispanic GDP was $2.6 trillion. If it were a standalone economy, it would be the 8th largest in the world. Our consumer market is $1.7 trillion.

Chapter 5: **Claudia Romo Edelman**

We're the youth - our median age is 28 years old, which is six years younger than the median in the entire country. Six in 10 Hispanics are millennials or younger. The most common age in our community is 11 years old compared to 58 for non-Hispanics.

We are the workforce of this country. We comprise 74% of new workers and 40% of the U.S. workforce growth. We are the taxpayers and the voters. In 2020, 31.5 million Hispanics are eligible to vote. We pay $215 billion in taxes and $100 billion in social security. We are entrepreneurs and job creators: 86% of all new jobs since the 2008 recession have been created by Hispanics. Latinas create small businesses six times faster than any other group in America.

And we will continue to grow, succeed, and increase these numbers because of our values. We believe in hard work. We have a deep commitment to our families. We are also ambitious and professional. We are fighters. We know how to overcome difficult situations. We are optimistic.

We are all of these things, and yet, we are underrepresented, misrepresented, and undervalued.

It makes no sense! We are powerful on paper but act weak; we are big but act small.

The Power of Marketing

I have been a marketer my entire life. In my experience, your goal is to highlight the best attributes of your product. Previously, I was doing this with global issues like poverty and AIDS to gain the hearts and minds of people and get them to volunteer time and donate money. The marketing around the Hispanic community does just the opposite; our best attributes are often hidden or downplayed, while others tell our stories and create a misconception of our strength and importance to the U.S. The result is that we are underrepresented, misrepresented, and undervalued. Not seen, not heard, not valued.

We have a 'reverse marketing problem.'

We Hispanics are born to shine, and we need to start controlling our narrative and highlighting the stories where we are fairly represented. We need to finally show people who we really are. We have a cloud covering our glow. But why? What are the barriers halting our progress? What stops our entrepreneurs from growing and scaling? Why are we not able to access our full potential?

If you are a marketer like me, you look for data to provide answers. I commissioned the Hispanic Sentiment Study as primary research to get some guidance. There are three main insights I found that are fundamental for our community's growth, and that have been the guiding light for our work and actions at the We Are All Human Foundation:

1. 77% of Hispanics don't know about their people's contributions to the country.
2. 76% of Hispanics have to pretend they're someone they're not in the workplace (Center for Talent Innovation).
3. 90% of Hispanics identify themselves as Hispanic but don't act as a community.

Considering that we are 100% Hispanic and 100% American, the We Are All Human Foundation created a platform to unify the

Chapter 5: **Claudia Romo Edelman**

community and showcase our incredible contributions to the country. With the help of a multimillion-dollar donation from one of the country's largest agencies, we created the Hispanic Star. The star symbol is a combination of the star, a well-known American symbol, and the eñe, a common accentuation for Spanish and Portuguese.

We needed a unifying platform - for Mexicans, Colombians, Venezuelans, Cubans, for all! Even for our allies. Think of the Rainbow for the LGBTQ. We want the Hispanic Star to become the symbol that shows we're united. But we also need to be seen as STARS. As stars of academia, sports, gastronomy - star workers, star friends, star consumers. Stars... part of the beautiful sky of this country.

We need to finally be seen, heard, and valued. I want every Hispanic to be proud and loud.

Every revolution, every big social movement throughout history starts with a group of people that believe in the same dream. We started with a group of 10, which then became 50, and now it's over 100 people and organizations. We have aligned Hispanic organizations and leaders to become the Hispanic Star Alliance. We went to the United Nations and revealed our plans. We invited a small group of companies, media, and allies to join forces and back this effort. Companies started joining, such as Procter and Gamble, IBM, Beam Suntory, Bristol Myers Squibb, SAP, NRG, YUM! Brands, U.S. Bank, LinkedIn, Buzzfeed, and critical mass will follow.

The Hispanic Star is a unification platform for Hispanics as employees, consumers, and community.

When COVID hit, the Hispanic Star jumped into action as it quickly became clear that COVID-19 disproportionately affected Hispanics at both the health and economic levels.

This unification platform morphed into a support system to communicate, organize, and mobilize our leadership, and to incentivize individuals and corporations to donate, volunteer, or share information to benefit Hispanics affected by COVID-19. At the community level, we organized Hispanic Star Hubs to support each other, taking action where their community needs it most. Already, these hubs have distributed more than 1.2 million products and helped more than 200,000 families nationwide.

I invite you all to take action, to do something. Wherever you are and whatever you do, there is something you can do to advance our community, to take a step toward making sure we are seen, heard, and valued. Everyone has a role to play. We will get there - paso a pasito - if every one of us takes even one small step, we will get there.

Use the framework of the Hispanic Star to guide your actions and be a guiding principle for this collective journey. Think of the Hispanic Star like the Sustainable Development Goals. The Hispanic Star is a wide and wonderful framework that allows you to express your commitment to Hispanics in a holistic approach. It will be beneficial to all to make sure the Hispanic Star is widely known, recognized, and respected.

Invest in it now and be a first mover. The Hispanic Star will become a global brand that represents Latino empowerment and demonstrates unity and pride.

Chapter 5: **Claudia Romo Edelman**

You can help us get there. Display it front and center! We have beautiful iconography, available to everyone - use it in windows, talking points, t-shirts - just like the SDGs or the rainbow during pride month. We want to see the Hispanic Star everywhere and for every Hispanic Heritage Month to be proud, loud, and unified, allowing Latinos and allies to express their support for our community.

The Hispanic Star is also a great way for companies to showcase their employees as Hispanic Stars and their company as a Hispanic-friendly organization. A Hispanic Star company celebrates its Hispanic Star employees and is where allies are aware and active supporters of diversity and inclusion. You can become an ally, mentor a Hispanic, lend a hand, encourage your Hispanic employees to shine, and shine a light.

Engage at the community level through the Hispanic Star Hubs. Be part of a group of people from different industries and sectors who care for each other and want to create intentional networks of support. If there is no Hispanic Star Hub in your city, create one! You need to help to make your city Hispanic-friendly to attract Latino talent!

And lastly, if you're Hispanic, allow yourself to shine. Dream big, and don't forget to speak up and ask for help. Talk to your peers. Tell them about who we are as a community, our values, and our way of being. Share how it helps us to be encouraged and mentored, and that role models matter because we need to see it to be it.

See yourself as a star. Take a look in the mirror. You are strong and powerful. Believe it. The more people know about their power and start feeling empowered, the easier it will be to elevate the playing field for our entire community. Take a look at your industry and see that you fit at the top - aim high and stand up. Take someone with you. Once you make it to a place, open the door so that someone else can come in. Share the access code, don't be afraid. There is not only one seat at the table because there is no table, just a country full of opportunities for all of us to shine. Engage with your Employee Resource Group (ERG), and engage with your community.

You don't need permission to justify your existence #sinpena #readytoshine. Look up, see the sky. That is where you belong, among the many beautiful stars shining - so, dream away.

America is made of stars, Hispanics are one of them. Together we shine.

CHAPTER 6

DEAL SENSE™: HOW TO IDENTIFY OPPORTUNITIES, BUILD RELATIONSHIPS, & DRIVE VALUE IN ANY DEAL

By **CYDNI TETRO**

I was sitting at a large conference room table in a swanky Beverly Hills hotel on a Sunday afternoon, ready to negotiate a strategic investment in our company. In the weeks before this meeting, our executive team determined the options that were best for our company. We knew what we wanted (and needed) in this strategic investment.

As CEO of the company, I sat at one end of the table, and the CEO of the strategic investment partners sat at the other end. A few minutes into our conversation, he looked at me and said, "What deal do you want? Do you want me to invest in your company, buy your company, or create a joint venture?" In that one moment, I paused. I suddenly worried that what we wanted didn't really match what was best for him. So, instead of responding with, "We want XYZ, and here is why…" I responded with, "Any of those options work for us. What is best for you?" But I was wrong. Our team had already discussed what we wanted and did not want. Yet at the moment that mattered, I did not trust my deal sense when I was asked.

Six months later, we did close a deal with that company. It was not the deal we wanted, and it was under different terms than we could have had. It wasn't the deal our company needed, and it cost us.

Deals happen every day in every business. They are created in every department by people in all types of roles (not just sales teams - that's a myth). A deal can be closing a new investment, creating a strategic partnership, acquiring a new vendor, building analyst relationships, partnering across business divisions, securing funding for a new project, or working with the board. No matter the size of the deal or the parties involved, the ability to sense the deal is the difference between simply making an agreement and creating the right strategic solution. Doing this requires more than mutual agreement - it takes deal sense.

Deal Sense: *The ability to perceive all of the variables that will impact your ability to close a deal.*

Deal sense is essential for business leaders, entrepreneurs, executives, managers, and leaders on all organizational levels. The stronger your deal sense is, the better you can navigate meetings, seize opportunities, capture the attention of partners, and accelerate the building of value-add relationships.

Five Key Skills

Building this type of deal sense comes from mastering five key skills. Together, these skills enable leaders to drive results and build strong business relationships.

Chapter 6: **Cydni Tetro**

1. Master Observation

"It does not do to leave a live dragon out of your calculations if you live near one." —J.R.R. Tolkien.

Mastering observation includes being able to control your emotions, look deeply at your surroundings, pay attention to non-verbal cues, listen to what is and is not being said, and pay attention to the environment surrounding the interaction.

One CEO shared how observation was important in their acquisition negotiations. The acquisition of the company was in its final step. About a week before the deal should have closed she got called into a one-on-one meeting with one of the lead negotiators from the acquirer. It was not a normal request and one that required her to observe the details, environment, and conversation. She watched for details like the fact that it was an in-person meeting, which required her to fly to the acquirer's location. It was over lunch, in a casual, yet public space. There was hesitation at the beginning of the business conversation. All of these details started to tell a story about concerns with the deal.

If she hadn't taken the time to observe the details, it would have been easy to assume the deal was still on track to close. But the details told a different story, which in turn had her asking, "Is there a risk that the deal won't close?" She discovered that the deal was almost dead and refocused her energy on reviving it. If she hadn't paid attention to words, actions, and behaviors, she would not have asked the right questions to steer the conversation in a direction that focused on recovering the deal. By observing, she was able to ask better questions, understand concerns, and provide a rich response.

Mastering observation is a skill that requires you to pay attention to all of the details around you, and to be more focused on those details than on yourself. It is a skill that requires focus, listening, self-control, attention to detail, understanding non-verbal cues, and controlling emotions. Mastering observation is critical to successful interactions and relationships.

2. Align Motivations

"Motivation is the art of getting people to do what you want them to do because they want to do it." —Dwight D. Eisenhower.

To develop the skill of being able to align motivations, you must be able to see the strategic value of the relationship and understand how tactics of successful execution work. When aligning motivations, details about how the partnership will operationalize, where resources are coming from, and how success will be measured are critical to understanding how both sides can best work together.

The head of business development in an AI startup was forming a strategic channel partnership. The AI company was just starting to scale revenue and the partnership would provide access to a strong customer channel. The relationship made complete sense from a market and channel perspective, and both companies really wanted to do the deal. They created the partnership and started working together. Very quickly it became apparent that there was major misalignment in motivations for doing the deal.

The AI company wanted customer acquisition and the partner to help drive revenue, and the partner wanted the visibility of having an AI solution. The two companies were misaligned about how they would accomplish the objectives, specifically around how they drive revenue for the AI company. The deal never produced results and was a frustrating ordeal for both sides. Strong deal sense means that the negotiator not only understands why the deal makes sense for them, but can go deeper and understand what it will take to successfully implement a deal that makes sense for the other side, too. You must ensure that both parties are aligned on incentives, results, measures of success, and management of risks. Whenever there is a breakdown around the motivations of a deal, the outcomes never realize their full potential.

To develop this skill, you must learn to ask questions that go deeper, anticipate the next steps after an agreement has been reached, understand what success means to both parties, and be willing to discuss the issues critical to aligning motivations.

3. Create Win-Win Solutions

"Win-win is a belief in the Third Alternative. It's not your way or my way; it's a better way, a higher way." –Stephen Covey.

Creating win-win solutions is a critical skill in having great deal sense. It means that there is a focus on how value is created for all parties. Win-win means understanding what can be compromised on and what cannot be, understanding the BATNA (best alternative for the negotiated agreement), and thinking through possible responses to your proposal.

A CEO of a tech startup needed to renegotiate a strategic customer partnership with a Fortune 100 company. The original deal financials were not working, and they could not make the current deal profitable. The startup was producing strong results for their customer, but the model wasn't sustainable. Armed with the data, results, and ideas for a sustainable business model, she headed in to negotiate a different deal.

Prior to the meeting, she had determined what a new deal needed to accomplish, outlined the key elements required to continue a successful relationship, and identified the impact the current partnership had on the business. In the meeting, she talked through these details - what was and wasn't working, and what needed to change about the arrangement. This led to a powerful brainstorming session about how to restructure the relationship in a way that could meet both parties' needs. She walked out of the meeting with a win-win solution, a deal that moved the relationship from $300k to over $2M. She walked into the meeting prepared, understanding the tradeoffs and risks to both sides, and with an open mind to find real value for both parties.

Being a creator of win-win solutions is a critical deal sense skill. When both parties find an arrangement for mutual benefit, the deal has sustainability and resiliency. This skill requires you to be open-minded and creative, and willing to adapt your thinking to find ways for both parties to achieve success.

4. Drive Outcomes

This deal sense skill focuses on how to drive outcomes and be strongly aligned with the outcome priorities of the other side. When negotiating a deal, every person knows what outcomes will create success for themselves. They might include objectives such as increasing profitability, decreasing costs, or increasing operational efficiency, all of which are important drivers for the business and decision-making framework. Often in a negotiation, outcomes need to be discovered. It is a critical skill to discover the driving outcomes of the other party so that you can formulate a successful strategy to meet both their objectives and your own.

The Chief Strategy Officer of a tech company shared an experience about a board that decided to change out the management of a company. The board made a critical mistake when they didn't assess the impact of the change on customers. The board made sweeping changes, terminating everyone on the leadership team. They didn't create a customer communication strategy, implement a transition plan, or ask for anything from the team that had been running the business. The board wanted growth outcomes but did not understand the business or metrics. They let their lack of experience cloud their ability to trust the team or drive the right conversations around outcomes. By not being focused on driving the right outcomes, their approach undermined multi-million-dollar relationships, lost the trust of employees, focused on the wrong variables, and destroyed all of the value the business had created over years in just a matter of months. Through the transition, the customers commented on the board's lack of deal sense, their lack of ability to understand what was motivating and driving the customers to work with the company. By not understanding the business outcomes that were important to the customers, the business lost customers and revenue.

Deal sense requires you to be a strong driver of outcomes. You must have the ability to understand what is important to the other party, and what drives them to work with you. You then must be able to map out the structure of the deal in such a way that the outcomes can be met. Deals cannot be formed if outcomes aren't part of the foundation.

5. Accelerate Value-Creation

"Companies that focus solely on competition will ultimately die. Those that focus on value creation will thrive." —Edward De Bono.

According to the dictionary, an accelerator is "a person or thing that causes something to happen or develop more quickly." Another important skill of deal sense is the ability to identify ways that value can be created quickly. This skill requires the ability to see the places where value is realized. If value takes a long time to create, often the opportunity cost is too high for the relationship to last.

The team at a 3D printing company had built a product line that allowed fans to scan their faces and receive a full-color 3D printed character from their favorite storylines – including Marvel. The company launched and immediately afterward an opportunity presented itself to launch with a national retailer and toy company for Superhero September. This was only 60 days away, but the team at the company understood that when an opportunity presents itself, accelerating the value and activating every resource in the company was worth the effort. Within the 60 days, a new product was created and launched in the national retailer. The results from the effort were so successful that it became the platform for adding additional retailers, content partners, and product lines across the country. What made it work was the executive team understanding how to accelerate value-creation. They understood that speed, smart execution, and delivering results would lead to the next phase of growth.

Accelerating value while understanding the cost and tradeoffs is a skill that is fundamental to forming relationships. The development of this deal sense skill is grounded in your ability to quickly identify opportunities, activate resources in response, and make tradeoffs as new information comes in. People are often afraid to make decisions too quickly, scared they do not have enough information, and that more research is needed to determine the right approach. That approach can lead to a loss of momentum or paralysis by analysis. Moving forward, accelerating opportunity and value, and continuing to make progress unlocks the potential, strengthens the relationship, and becomes a foundation for success.

Deal sense requires the development of all five of these skills. When used together, the skills enable powerful deals, strategic projects, impactful results, and united teams. Deal sense, like all senses, can be improved, focused, refined, and strengthened. All leaders, internally and externally, can use their deal sense for successful results and relationships.

CHAPTER 7

THE PATH TO YOUR PURPOSE: DIRECTIONS AND DECISIONS

By **DENISA AXHAMI**

I asked a friend, "What should I do?"

"Denisa, you should do what is best for you," he reminded me.

It was at that moment I realized I was seeking answers from everyone but myself. This was ironic, as only I had the answers. Perhaps I was subconsciously seeking validation more than anything, but I was unaware of it. My reality was a daily constant pull from one career path to another. At the time, I was in graduate school at Michigan State University pursuing my master's degree in Social Work. I did not want to continue, but I refused to label myself a college dropout. After I sought answers within myself, I realized my true calling and purpose was in business, proudly referring to myself as an entrepreneur. Prior to withdrawing from graduate school to pursue what I loved, finding my purpose was a daily battle that drained me. Frustrated and conflicted, I searched everywhere for some sort of direction, unaware that it would make matters even worse. In simple terms, I was lost.

At certain points in life, you will find yourself feeling lost and seeking direction. We all do, but especially leaders. Leaders do not follow, and when following is not an option, it is up to the leaders to decide what is next. Through my own trial and error, I learned lessons from mistakes that people, especially those in business, should be aware of. One of the biggest mistakes to make is approaching the wrong people to seek advice. Emphasis on "wrong." I say this with personal experience and justified reasoning. See, you cannot compare your path to someone else's path. What may have been an excellent decision for one person may be a poor decision for you. On the contrary, another person's "closed door" they warn you about may be a door you unknowingly have the key to. However, the right people will be your support systems, such as counselors and mentors. Ultimately, it is you that makes the decisions.

You have your own path to get to your purpose, and I will prepare you for the directions and decisions you must make along the way. Since words alone cannot capture this guide, you must visually picture yourself walking down your path to your purpose - literally. You will see signs, dead ends, green and greener grass, endure all types of weather, obstacles, and get tired along the way. But there is good news. You will reach your destination, and that destination is your purpose. Let's begin.

Preparing For the Journey

Being prepared for what is to come is crucial, as this will be no easy task. Are you ready? I mean really ready? Visualize this: If dedication was water, you will not go far without it. If a plan was a pair of shoes, you will not be able to walk without stability. Most importantly, if preparation was a map, you will get lost without it. The preparation stage may make or break the completion of the path you are about to take. Various steps will assist you with the preparation stage, such as gathering a support system and developing positive self-care routines. For example, I bought books for businesswomen and set time

Chapter 7: **Denisa Axhami**

for meditation to ensure I was prepared to take on major responsibilities. Without mental, spiritual, and physical strength, you will not be able to focus on the destination: your purpose.

Before your first step, you must decide on the first direction you will take. You do not want to take a turn that will lead you to a dead end, for example. This is why it is important to be wise and observe your surroundings before you take that very step. I failed to do so myself, and I ended up lost and forced to go back to where I started. I took a careless first step and got in the habit of spontaneous decisions. I did not look at my surroundings, such as the oversaturated industry, and invested money in the wrong areas. My young age likely played a part in this "nothing will happen to me" mentality I had at the time. It was a false reality that my business would stand out from the millions of others, and that my funds would come right back when I generate a ton of money. This was unrealistic, and I did not pay attention. While I was not paying attention, I ran into obstacles I was not prepared to overcome and I learned my lesson on the importance of the first step the hard way.

Here is how to decipher the direction your first step will follow. For one, do not go backward. The goal is to get closer to the destination, and this requires you to either move forward, left, or right. Of the three directions, go with the one you are most comfortable with. Let's visualize this. If the path on the left has visible obstacles, avoid it. If the path in front of you is crowded with people (saturated competition), reconsider that route. You do not want to have obstacles and a large amount of competition this early on. After listing the pros and cons, you will likely make the decision to take the right direction, no pun intended.

Enduring the Weather

There is no umbrella to protect you from the rainy days that lie ahead. You will have to endure it all, especially the storms life brings each of us. It will be difficult to find the strength to continue, but there is really no choice. Whether you continue on or return to the starting line during hard times, it will be through the rain or storm. Be mentally, spiritually, and physically prepared for this in the preparation stage before even taking the first step in the right direction. I was not prepared in that manner, and I broke down several times. Ultimately, I headed back to my starting line. That was difficult to experience in and of itself. The disappointment in myself was unbearable, but as a natural-born leader, I knew I would come back even stronger. Each person has unique ways to strengthen themselves mentally, spiritually, and physically. For me, it was prayer, reading, and running. There will be rainy days, but a little rain never stopped a runner.

Stop Signs

On your path, there will be "stop signs." These stop signs symbolize pauses you may have to take which are not in your control. Examples of these may be finances, an unexpected illness, or even life in general. We cannot control anything except our reactions to the situation. During this time, we must look around, be cautious, and proceed when it is clear to safely continue.

When we reach "stop signs" on our path to our purpose, it gives us the ability to take a break. As frustrating as waiting may seem, it is actually an opportunity to rest. A bad habit I had once I began my journey was rushing too fast and disregarding life's symbolic stop signs. I wanted to find success quickly, but that is not realistic. In real life, if we do not observe stop signs or make the decision to disregard them, we are in immediate danger. Just like the danger and disaster running a stop sign in real life possesses, my career faced the same fate of destruction had I not been so lucky. One symbolic stop sign I experienced was health-related. I was not in the best health, but I wanted to continue. It was frustrating that I could not move forward until I was healthy again. I tried to take on the responsibilities of running a business alone but did more harm than good. If you rush and disregard these symbolic stop signs on your path to your purpose, you risk losing it all, forced to pick up the pieces. Once the road is clear, you can continue your journey.

Dead Ends

Dead ends are inevitable. Committing to a route that ultimately leads to a dead end will feel greatly discouraging. A few examples are negative feedback, a lack of sales, or a poor business structure. You may tell yourself "there is no way out" or "I cannot do this." But a dead end does not mean your journey is over or that your path ends there. By hitting a dead end, you are even closer to your destination, since you now know what direction not to take. It will give you a chance to strategize things differently. In fact, we may see signs of a dead end ahead of time, and this gives us a chance to turn right around and redirect ourselves. This is similar to a real-life situation. In my experience, my dead end was the lack of sales. This dead end left me doubting my product and my marketing tactics, but most importantly, funds were in jeopardy. I had to restrategize. I learned what not to do. In real life, we do not just stand at a dead end wondering if we'll ever get out, so why do so when you hit dead ends on your path to your purpose?

The Greener Grass

"The grass is greener on the other side," is a quote that symbolizes the belief that one side is better than the other. It is interesting how we human beings compare our "grass" to someone else's. To better explain this, let's have grass symbolize a person's success. I mention this to remind you, the reader, that sometimes the grass is not real. It may be a false foundation to allow others to think that they are successful, when in reality it is all an illusion. Do not compare yourself to others. Your destination on the path to your purpose may not have beautiful green grass at first. It is your job to water and care for your own grass rather than envy your neighbors.

Obstacles

Unlike stop signs, you can maneuver around obstacles, no matter how big or small. What may stop you from overcoming obstacles is fear. Career-wise, fear is a result of the lack of faith in a person's abilities. A common minor obstacle you may face is discouragement from others. This can be overcome by focusing on your support system, rather than clinging to discouraging comments. The major obstacles are ones that are difficult to overcome, but with careful steps, a leap of faith, and savings, you will overcome them. I faced these obstacles myself. I felt my business structure was unsteady and burdened, so I carefully cut down on workload. My faith began to weaken, so I began encouraging my own self to continue. When funds were an issue, I would slow down or even seize operations until I was financially ready to continue. These are some ways to maneuver around obstacles in the way of our destination.

You Will Get Tired

Your endurance will be greatly tested. There will be periods where you lose track of time and push your limits farther than ever. As unbelievable as it sounds, the longest shift I have ever worked was a total of 73 hours. No sleep, no coffee, no breaks. 73 hours of unpaid work my future depended on. Today's most successful individuals in the world will tell you that sleep was never a priority. I am not discouraging rest, but rather preparing you for the sleepless nights, exhaustion, and mental states where you no longer feel as if there is a light at the end of the tunnel, or as if you will never reach your destination - as if you will never find your purpose. I am here to remind you that there is good news. You will find your purpose.

Your Purpose

Past all that you will encounter on your path, your purpose awaits. All of the signs, dead ends, greener grass, obstacles, rainy days, and exhaustion lead you further in the right direction. Throughout this journey, you will learn what turns to avoid, where to focus your energy, how to overcome burdens, and find strength within yourself you did not realize you possessed. Most importantly, you will recognize what kept you going. The thing that will keep you motivated throughout the entire process is super important. In my personal experience, it is my entrepreneurial spirit that has fueled my fire. I eventually realized my purpose was something I had rooted within me my entire life. I am a leader. I lead people. I have learned to lead people throughout many paths, one being a path to find one's purpose.

To conclude this chapter, I encourage you to ask yourself why. You must identify your specific purpose and why you have decided to follow a path toward it. Perhaps you enjoy a challenge or seek adventures, or in my case, paving ways to eventually lead others. Whatever the reason, the answer to your "why" reflects the answer to the "what should I do?" question. My answer to you, the one about to embark on the path to their purpose, is that you should do what is best for you.

CHAPTER 8

GNOTHI SEAUTON (KNOW THYSELF): LESSONS FROM A GLOBAL MUSIC PRODUCER

By **KRYSTALÁN CHRYSSOMALLIS**

There's an ancient Greek saying, "gnothi seauton," meaning "know thyself," which my father taught me and has been my guiding truth for so long. From Aeschylus to Socrates to Plato, the wisest early philosophers believed that true peace and prosperity came from within and that everything starts from the self – and as Aristotle said, "Knowing yourself is the beginning of all wisdom." The Greeks even inscribed "Gnothi Seauton" in stone on the forecourt of the Temple of Apollo at Delphi, to be an everlasting tribute to their philosophy, which they knew would outlast even their own culture and civilization, holding lessons for the future.

As a global music producer, much of my life has been an exhilarating whirlwind, living in and experiencing some of the most exciting and unusual locations in the world, where I have been so fortunate to encounter and learn from new cultures, people, and places. I've put on some of the biggest shows in the business, set in more than 60 countries, from a two-night show before the 4,500-year-old Great Sphinx of Giza in Egypt featuring a live video broadcast from the International Space Station to concerts in the world's most beautiful and historic settings. From the ancient cities of Byblos and Amman to

Puerto Rican castles and royal Indian palaces, from China's Forbidden City and Russia's Kremlin to one of my favorite places: the unexplored splendor of AlUla, Saudi Arabia.

In all of these places and in the countless settings in between, I have been guided by this philosophy of my ancestors. "Know thyself" has taught me the importance of falling in love with who you are and who you are becoming, and how the journey of discovering oneself is a beautiful thing that provides meaning and truth in itself. The better you "know thyself," the easier it is to see your strengths, weaknesses, values, and goals and ultimately to see the path that leads to a rich and fulfilling life. Indeed, once we know what a meaningful life looks like for us, we can begin to pursue it: purging the toxic decisions that distract us from our journey and pursuing new paths that lead to being fulfilled.

"Know thyself" is also about emotional intelligence; the ability to understand how your emotions and your perceptions or beliefs may be influencing your thinking and behavior or decision-making is a huge benefit in life and in business. Stopping to ask "why" you are doing what you do and why you are thinking as you are helps guide decision-making and ultimately, may prompt you to change and create something completely different. Once you are able to articulate what is important for you, it helps you then be able to see that in others.

In my own journey, gnothi seauton has taught me so many lessons for success in my industry and in my personal life, including embracing the power of gratitude and mindfulness, learning how to ask empowering questions, teaching myself to trust my art and create my own benchmarks of success, and also how to challenge my thoughts and resist complacency, which I believe is the death of creativity.

When doing business internationally, the concept of "know thyself" has been absolutely critical – as I believe it can be for anyone who travels or works abroad. "Know thyself" has helped guide my questions and ability to understand any new culture I was immersed in. When committed to questioning your own thoughts and being mindful of your goals and priorities, you can't help but listen more and learn from others, instead of talking or telling. When negotiating a deal, you are better equipped to identify what is really driving the other side of the table, and then you can address it in a manner where both sides come out feeling like they got what they needed and ultimately, close the deal.

Most importantly, pursuing a life of knowing oneself teaches us to ask new questions and learn new lessons so we can continue to develop as we go down our career paths and our lives. Constant questioning is the foundation of growth and, therefore, of success. Recognizing that you don't know everything and always have a lot to learn, no matter how far along your path may be, is as important as it can be humbling. And with humility also comes a newfound ability to be tolerant, accepting, honest, and open.

From a business perspective, acceptance and tolerance are critical. As our global markets expand, as our planet becomes smaller and smaller and we are sharing space with other cultures, it's important to embrace tolerance: of the new people and places you encounter, the partners and clients you work with, and, of course, the teams you build. I believe that not only learning how to accept our differences but celebrating them and building upon each other's strengths can lead to some of the strongest teams in the world. It's the blending of each person's unique background that strengthens the whole.

Of course, embracing gnothi seauton is not a static process, something we do once and are complete. I believe that it is so important to accept that we will not always have the answers and that this is always an ongoing process. There is a beautiful passage in Rainer Maria Rilke's Letters To A Young Poet, in which the author advises a young man: "Be patient toward all that is unsolved in your heart and try to love the questions themselves, like locked rooms and like books that are now written in a very foreign tongue. Do not now seek the answers, which cannot be given you because you would not be able to live them. And the point is, to live everything. Live the questions now. Perhaps you will then gradually, without noticing it, live along some distant day into the answer."

Gnothi seauton can be more than the foundation for changing yourself – it can be the foundation for changing the world. The more we know and love ourselves, the brighter we shine to the world, and the better we can share our gifts. For me, personally and professionally, one of the things I am most passionate about is that we are all connected, we are all one. Music and the arts give us ways of expressing this, visualizing it and connecting us with others allows us to transcend all borders and limitations we place on ourselves in a fluid and seamless way. They connect, they heal, and they go right for your heart and soul. Art can make us laugh, cry, and be inspired, no matter what career we choose, the language we speak, or the country we live in. They can inspire joy, sympathy, sadness, fear, comfort, or any other emotion.

Chapter 8: **Krystalán Chryssomallis**

The belief in the unifying and healing power of the arts is why I am passionate about taking my work to some of the most unexplored corners of the globe, including Russia, China, Saudi Arabia, and Egypt, particularly for Westerners. Often, for political reasons, we overlook certain places, but we do so at the expense of so much beauty and even our common humanity. A happy instrumental song receives the same exuberant response from a person in India as it does in Saudi Arabia, Brazil, or Greece. Music makes the world a little smaller, helping us acknowledge, appreciate, and even celebrate the common humanity we share.

For that same reason, I became an avid photographer. My first camera was given to me by my father at an early age, and I soon began carrying it everywhere, capturing the energy and emotion of concerts, and then the beauty and isolation of the night sky and the personal narratives that come with photojournalism. The storytelling power of a photograph and how it can freeze a moment in time, capture the energy and essence of a significant experience, and transport the viewer to feel it with you is incredible to me. Just like music, photographs give us a way to connect with others and make the world a little smaller, helping us acknowledge, appreciate, and even celebrate the common humanity we share. Through the power of a photograph, we can see that we simply are not that different from each other.

When I was on assignment for photography in Africa, I had a moment where a lion, the king of the jungle, taught me what "know thyself" really looks like. I was in an open Jeep, stopped to take in the beauty of the open plains when a lion spotted our vehicle and began walking ever so slowly toward us. I knew this lion could see me. In fact, he was looking right through to my soul. He continued to lock eyes with me, never breaking his gaze as he continued to walk toward me, so close I could have touched him. As he circled around and took a comfortable seat and continued to stare right through me, I realized why this animal is indeed the king of the jungle. A lion is a lion, no matter what happens to him; no matter what he endures or goes through, he will never lose sight of who and what he is. Because of this, he held all of the power. Because his power is within. It was a lesson for me, to never lose sight of who I am. So, as I move forward in life and career, I will forever remember this lion who taught me the importance of "know thyself."

My journey isn't a typical one. But it is beautiful because it is just that: a journey. One in which I am always striving, seeking, and learning. We must resist the tendency to reduce ourselves to that which we do now, to our careers and the skill sets we currently use, without realizing that we contain multitudes, and have so much value to contribute to the world. We all have so much potential to share with the world if only we have the courage to pursue the best and most true versions of ourselves.

I encourage all people in business, no matter their industry, to find the courage to ask what mark they want to make on the world, and what special talent within themselves that the world needs. Untap the creativity that lies within you by practicing gratitude, asking empowering questions, living intentionally, and trusting in your talents. And then share that beauty with the world. As Ralph Waldo Emerson said, "This world is but a canvas to our imagination." Have the courage to paint in every color.

CHAPTER 9

TURNING PASSION INTO YOUR PURPOSE

By **DR. LORI HADDAD**

I have spent much of my career mentoring other people and being mentored and helped by others. Finding out who you are, what you are passionate about, and how to turn that into a career is not a singular, linear thing. It takes teamwork and collaboration; being open to others and asking for help can change your life.

Whether it is for one individual or in a time of global crisis, teamwork and collaboration and compassion are extremely important.

One fantastic example of this is when a young man came to me at the hospital last year. Eric had been a college basketball player and he went to medical school. When I met him, he was miserable in his residency for interventional radiology. It just wasn't what he wanted anymore but with med school debt looming over him, he didn't think he had any other option but to continue on the path he was on.

I get it. Debt can be debilitating and it can guide you on a path or journey you aren't passionate about. At one time, I had a lot of debt and it was difficult and took a long time, but I was able to use my gifts and talents to identify paths to getting out from under the debt to pursue my passions.

Eric was very interested in trying to pursue dermatology, but it wasn't his specialty and dermatology is one of the hardest residencies to get. There was no way he could quit his radiology residency and just hope to find one in dermatology, he needed his job and the money. I could clearly see Eric's passion and his talent, and I had a way for him to collaborate with me where I could mentor him and help him identify a new path.

I had done a ton of research on products for acne-related disorders. I had studies and data and hundreds of pages of research and information and I wrote a paper, I just did not have the time to actually put it all together to have it published. I offered to have Eric organize my research and assist with writing a second paper that needed full write-up, a project about blood clotting disorders I was passionate about personally. He'd be a co-author on two articles when it was published.

Eric spent months working with the research, writing, revising, and working with me to get the two papers done and published. I needed the projects finished because of the credibility and validity it would give my organic safe-for-all-skin-types skincare line of products I developed, and proof that an underlying genetic mutation, the MTHFR mutation, was the underlying cause of not only blood clots, but much more. Eric needed the experience, as he didn't have anything dermatology-related on his resume to make him attractive to the competitive residencies.

It's about teamwork. We worked together toward our shared goals and it benefitted both of us. This is what true mentorship is. It is not instant gratification or demanding what you want, but finding a way to work with others to accomplish your goals and potentially identify a new path.

Now that the paper has been published, Eric has been able to land several interviews for prestigious dermatology residencies! He put in a lot of work, effort, energy, and time around his current residency and life obligations to learn and go after what he wanted and now his career has shifted to a new path - one he is extremely excited about.

Not only was I able to see Eric's gifts and talents, but I was also able to help him identify them for himself and drive himself forward with patience and hard work.

This is my legacy. Mentoring others and collaboration is incredibly rewarding. It just goes to show that your legacy matters. Your time here on Earth matters, and especially as women, our platform and mentoring are important. People Matter.

It is all a balance. Sometimes you cannot pursue your passion because you aren't sure what your passion is yet or you don't have the right experience yet or you haven't clarified your priorities. Whatever the reason, now is the time to jump in with both feet and find what makes you happy and also makes a difference to others.

Finding Your Passion

Many times, on the way to finding your passion, you are driven down one path and even if it's a path you've been on for five or 10 years, you suddenly find yourself unhappy. It is no longer your passion - or maybe it never was. And if you are not passionate about it, you will not persevere.

You will always get the best return on your investment when you are truly passionate about what you're doing. An example of this passion is this book. When I was looking into being a part of this book, one of the questions on the application was "Why do you want to be part of this book?"

For my father, it came down to leaving a legacy. My father always wanted to write a book and as an elderly man with some health struggles, many people questioned if he could or should do it. But it was a driving force in him and he wanted to share his story, his experiences as a Marine in Iwo Jima during World War II, and his passion for his Lebanese heritage, food, and culture. My father is living proof that no matter what challenges you face, you can still do something you love. By the way, his published book is called *I'm Possible: the Mediterranean Diet Lebanese Cookbook* by Ayoub David Haddad. Bon appétit habibi!

I am writing this chapter as part of the first-ever all-women *Mission Matters* book because I have a gift for helping people realize they don't need to be stuck. That they can evolve and change and find the thing they are passionate about and then succeed. And not just in work but in life, as a human being, with family and friends everything else life has to offer. Finding your passion drives you to work harder to succeed and opens doors to diversifying and expanding your experience. My reason is that I love helping people and giving back by educating others and helping them identify their next path.

Figuring Out What Defines You

The first step to finding your passion and your purpose is knowing who you are and digging in to discover and define your identity and talents.

Chapter 9: **Dr. Lori Haddad**

For me, I never let circumstances or other people define me. God is in control and He created me to fulfill a mission. Knowing my identity and mission is important and allows me to ignore any people who may try to tear me down or knock me off of my path.

When I am working with other people, the first thing I have them do is quietly reflect on what they are good at, what other people think they are good at, and what makes them happy. I have them write it down on paper and look at each thing and think about whether it can be an option to pursue to make money. For each option, I have them think about who out in the world could be an example of someone using that skill or talent to make money and how they might be able to look at that person's path and model it out for themselves.

When creating this list, it is important to be honest and self-critical. There may be things you like and are interested in but that you aren't actually good at or could make money with. You have to self-analyze and reflect on what YOU are good at to identify your specific talents, skills, and gifts.

Ask yourself things like "What am I happiest doing?" and "Am I good enough at this or can I get good enough at this to master it and make money?" and "Am I willing to go back to school or take courses or lessons to get to that point of mastery?"

Once you have your list of skills and talents, mark them in order of priority. Which thing is most important to you or that you're best at? Which one(s) could be a potential career path? Then pick one to three of them and focus on them to become your new passion and purpose. Own them.

Turning Your Passion Into Your Purpose

You have to truly own your skills and passions. You can't be self-deprecating or feel like it is arrogant to be good at something and proud of it. Work on your confidence, whether that is improving your skills through practice and learning or doing the "fake it 'til you make it" confidence strategy.

You can't turn your passion into a purpose until you know it is something you can commit to and pursue long-term and with diligence.

Moving into your passion is the opposite of survival mode. Survival mode is when you ignore your passions and purpose to do what you have to to survive and pay the bills. The process of finding your passion and making it your purpose and a new path is moving from just surviving to doing what you love while surviving.

Try out different careers and options to see what you really enjoy or don't like and will not pursue. You don't have to interview and get a new job to learn this. Asking questions and trying different things helps you clarify what you want and don't want. I actually traveled and met my role models so I could learn from people and actively sought people out to learn from. They helped me find my passion and your mentors will help you find yours.

There are many ways you can try out different things, such as:
- Shadowing someone in that career for a day to see what their days are like.
- Call or walk into a facility, introduce yourself, and ask for help in defining what the job does and all it involves.

Chapter 9: **Dr. Lori Haddad**

- Take a class in-person or online on the subject to dive in deeper and learn more.
- Potentially look for freelance clients in that subject area to try doing it professionally and see if you like it. Even with amateur experience, you can find freelance clients at average rates to see if working professionally in that field is a good fit.

Most people, especially those who love their job, are happy to help others see if their job is the right one for them. They love what they do so they want to show others their passion. Don't be afraid to ask for help and support - another reason teamwork and collaboration is important. Finding someone who models the career path you want will be an amazing resource for you. Look for mentors who can help you now and remember to pay it forward and BE a mentor to others as you settle and grow in your career.

Don't be afraid to talk to strangers in the field you're interested in and introduce yourself. Networking is very important in every industry. My son is getting a degree in Sports Management and by happenstance, my handyman, who is from Romania, also works for the attorney for the Detroit Pistons. He offered to connect my son with the attorney! This is just one example of being open to networking and meeting all kinds of people and being open to connecting.

Just remember, learning who you are and what you want is a journey in itself. You might fail and that is okay. You might find something you love is not a viable career path and that is okay. Failure and trials and tribulations are part of the journey and no one has success without some failures along the way.

It's about owning your skills and confidence and finding what makes you happy - even if that doesn't end up being your job. It's also a balance and you need to create clear boundaries to foster happiness. You want to find ways to not bring work home with you and balance your job and passions with your life and downtime.

Owning Your Purpose

Once you've learned more and narrowed down your passions into one or two you want to pursue, it's time to take action steps. That might be getting a degree, license, or certification or it might be interviewing for jobs in that field. Either way, it's time to control your own destiny. You have to be proactive and be your own best advocate for what you want.

Learning is a lifelong process and you never really feel "ready" to jump in, but you have to do it. And learning can come from anywhere. I've had mentors who were decades younger than me and I've mentored people older than me. It's not about age, it"s about their specialty and expertise. You can learn from everyone around you.

Keep your eyes on the prize and focus as much as you can on what you want and your purpose. Make every attempt to decrease stress and the things that make you anxious and keep you from your goal. The number one issue that causes stress is money.

The best way to decrease your stress about money is to diversify. Diversify your jobs, talents, and portfolio. For example, I have not just been a doctor with my own practice. I've been a consultant, a product designer, a public/motivational speaker, an author, a house flipper, and more. Look for opportunities to create additional income streams or be an entrepreneur. Even working from home, these days technology has made it easier than ever to work from home and make money even while in school, such as with writing for clients, social media management, and more. The technology allows you to learn and work in so many new ways.

When you diversify, it's also important to be able to know when to get out. If it's not working or you're not making money, don't keep knocking your head into the way. Toss that idea and work on a new one. Don't allow yourself to be trapped in one thing. Every breath is important, don't waste your time and energy and breath when something isn't right for you. Use it as a learning experience to move forward.

Be excited! Your passion makes you happy, which positively impacts other people and your own excitement often will lead to new opportunities and more money. Remember to have a team of support, mentors, and those who encourage you and propel you forward.

Passion Moves You

As you work through identifying your passions, gaining confidence and mastery, and then putting those skills to work for you, you are never on your own. It's important to collaborate with others and find mentors who can help you learn and role models who are doing what you want to do. Being able to work with others toward your goal will help you visualize what you are really working toward.

And when you get to the point of living your purpose, make sure you pay it forward. Mentor others, whether that is through mentoring programs or one-on-one. Help others develop their own passions and purpose and talents. Age and experience level doesn't matter, we can all learn from everyone in this world. Let every day be a learning experience.

If I hadn't had - and still have - an excellent team around me to work with and learn from, I do not think I would be where I am today: Happy, successful, diversified, and filled with passion and purpose.

CHAPTER 10

GETTING PERSONAL WITH FINANCE

By **MARGUERITA CHENG**

When I participated in *Money Matters Business Leaders volume 2*, I wrote about the many different faces of confidence. I once had a manager tell me I "asked too many questions" and "spent too much time building relationships" and that those things made me appear less confident. He, of course, was a loud, gregarious, almost arrogant brand of confidence, while mine is quieter and steeped in connections with people.

If you define confidence the way he does, then I probably do appear to lack it. But I define confidence as the ability to learn, ask questions, dive deeper, form relationships with clients, and admit when I am wrong. The beautiful thing is that we can both be right. Everyone's confidence is their own.

Confidence and resilience are crucial in business, especially as a woman. There are societal pressures and expectations on women that we have to be a certain way, act a certain way, and raise our kids in a specific way. That we can't "have it all."

What I've learned is that as you grow and change, your wants and needs change. Your definition of "having it all" changes, too. What I wanted in my 20s was completely different than what I want now in my 40s. My confidence has evolved, my career, my relationships, as a mother, everything. I've learned you can never let others tell you what you "should" be or whether or not you're confident enough. I guess I want to say that as I have evolved, so has my confidence

If I'd let that one manager be right, I would not be the successful entrepreneur I am today.

Regardless of age, relationship status, ethnicity, socioeconomic status, location - every woman deserves the opportunity to become not just confident and resilient but **financially** confident and resilient. This drives me every single day in my work as a financial planner. I love working with young people or those new to financial planning and teaching them how to look at money differently and plan for their goals.

How Did I Get Here?

I am an ABC: American-born Chinese. My father was born in China and left there to pursue higher education and serve in the military in Taiwan, before eventually applying to grad school in the United States and ending up in Wisconsin. After school, he moved to New York, where he met my mother.

One piece of advice my father gave has stuck with me my entire life: "Never measure your self-worth by your net worth," and he stressed the importance of investing in education and knowledge.

As an undergraduate student, I pursued double degrees in East Asian Studies and Finance. I won a scholarship to work and study

Chapter 10: **Marguerita Cheng**

in Tokyo, Japan, where I got my first corporate finance. Eventually, I moved back to the U.S., met my husband, got a house, and had three beautiful kids.

I joined the financial planning profession in 1999 and completed the requirements for CFP® certification in 2004, and gave birth to my third child in early 2005. All the while, I was working in finance, building my credibility, authority, and experience. I continued to work for large finance firms until 2013. It was then that I made the move to become a financial planner and start my own business, Blue Ocean Global Wealth.

One thing that became important to me and pushed me toward entrepreneurship was wanting to educate and teach people about personal finance and make it less intimidating and overwhelming for people. In large financial firms, they had minimum amounts that people could invest or bring into the company. A young couple might have a life savings of $35,000 and want to invest it and learn about personal wealth management, and some firms would turn them away because they didn't meet the company's initial minimum required amount.

It's true that many financial planners just look at the size of the investment portfolio, but what sets me apart is my empathy and confidence that I can help anyone who wants to learn. People come to my office and share their personal stories, their hardships and difficulties, and they want to learn about how to become financially resilient, save, invest, and plan for their futures. In most cases, everyone is doing the best they can with the information they have, and asking for help can be vulnerable. I want to emphasize that asking for help is a sign of courage.

That is why I love my job. I get to help others, teach, and get to know amazing people on their path to financial literacy and success.

4 Tips for Planning Your Financial Future

When it comes to learning about financial planning, there are a few things to think about. My approach differs from the industry norm but I find that personal touch and empathy go a long way in instilling confidence in people.

Plan For Tomorrow, But Enjoy Today

You hear it all the time: "Just save more!" Yes, I am rolling my eyes. Everyone knows saving money is important. It's like being told we should eat healthier or exercise more. We KNOW, we just don't always know HOW.

Many financial planners and wealth managers seem to just lecture their clients. "Save more money! Stop spending! You'll never reach your goals!"

I like to adopt a different approach. Instead of telling my clients they need to be saving money, we identify their long and short-term goals and priorities, and then have a deep discussion to review their current expenses. We can see how much money is being spent daily, weekly, monthly, and annually on things like rent or mortgage, groceries, dining, fun, and other expenses.

This exercise helps clients understand their cash flow, clients can identify opportunities to reduce expenses and "find" cash flow to fund their goals and dreams. For example, a client may be paying $160 per month for cable, internet, and a landline bundle, but realize they only ever watch streaming services and only have the landline for the cost savings. By switching to internet service only, they save over $100 per month. Or a client may see the cumulative effect of ordering less takeout or minimizing rideshare expenses. Small changes make a big difference over time when it comes to financial planning.

It can feel like you have to "give up" things you enjoy to save, but really it's about cutting back, not cutting things out completely. You don't want to cut out everything you enjoy - it's important to still live your life! And as I tell my clients, temporarily cutting back can go a long way when planning your future and reaching your goals.

When you fully understand and articulate your goals and priorities, you're better able to find ways you can make small changes today to have a more secure future.

Many of my clients have never had a written budget or seen all their expenses laid out like this, and it is an incredibly useful tool.

Retire TO Something

A really great way to think of retirement planning is that you are retiring TO something, not FROM everything. In order to have something to retire to, you have to make a plan now. It feels far away today, but life moves quickly!

I have one client who decided he wanted to take piano lessons after retiring from work. Another wanted to start a boutique cake business. One wanted to volunteer doing career coaching for women. Another wanted to provide reliable transportation to senior citizens to help them get to medical appointments in a safe and efficient manner. Another one uses his skills as a pharmacist to go on medical mission trips in West Africa.

Whatever your dreams or plans are for retirement, you have to plan for an income during that time. Whether you plan to travel, play music, write a book, learn to dance, or volunteer more, you still will have bills to pay.

Once you understand where your money is currently going and identify ways you can potentially cut back, it's time to develop a spending plan and budget and start saving money for your short-term emergency fund and invest in long-term ways for retirement.

You definitely need a short-term emergency fund. It's the money you'll spend if you have unexpected medical bills or need to fix your car or you lose your job. You do not want to be dipping into this fund each month to go out on a date night or grab a new pair of shoes.

So, here is how I approach this: After reviewing the budget and spending plan, we look at how much money is left over each month. This is not "disposable" income, you're not throwing it away, it's the remaining cash flow left at the end of the month. Let's say it is $400.

We're going to take the leftover total and split it in half, as things happen and you may go over your spending plan by a few dollars or something comes up. So, you are committing to saving $200. Of that $200, $100 will go to your emergency savings and the other $100 will go to long-term investing.

It is important to not overcommit to savings. If you usually have $300 left at the end of the month, don't push yourself to commit $400 to savings. When you over-commit and then do not meet that goal, it's easy to become frustrated and discouraged with the whole process. It can even lead you to stop trying to save at all! Even if it is $20 to savings and $20 to invest, you ARE making a difference and are getting closer to your goals every single month.

What Should You Be Investing In?

If you have access to a retirement account such as a 401(k) through your employer, then absolutely do it. Many companies match contributions up to a certain percent, so take advantage of that. It's free money!

If you do not have access to a 401(k) or are a freelancer, you can set up your own retirement plan. IRAs can easily be opened online with either custodians or mutual fund companies. Some examples are Charles Schwab, Merrill Edge, TD Ameritrade, Fidelity, American Funds, and Vanguard. Some providers do not require an initial minimum investment, but if you have a lump sum to get you started, that's good, too. With an IRA, you can keep your money as cash or invest it into mutual funds.

When setting up an IRA, look at your spending and savings plan and simply create an automatic deposit into your IRA from your checking account each month with half of the money you have earmarked for savings.

You can choose which kind of IRA you want, both are great and you can have both or one of them. Whatever works best for your situation is how you want to choose. For example, a SEP IRA is great if you want to save money now and pay taxes when you remove it later. With a Roth IRA, the money you are putting into it has already been taxed, so you pay the tax on it now and then do not have to pay taxes on it when you take the money out in retirement. For 2020, with a Roth IRA, you can put in up to $6,000 per year or $7,000 if you are over 50. As a note, there are annual income limits: If you are married and filing separately, single, or filing as the head of household, you can contribute to a Roth IRA in 2020 up to the limit for your age if your modified adjusted gross income (MAGI) is less than $124,000. The amount you can contribute is reduced if your MAGI is between $124,000 and $139,000; If your MAGI exceeds $139,000, you cannot contribute to a Roth IRA. For a self-employed individual, SEP IRA contributions are limited to 25% of your net earnings from self-employment (not including contributions for yourself), up to $57,000 for 2020.

Retirement accounts are not your only investment opportunities, though they are a great place to start. For some people, homeownership makes sense. Basically, it comes down to your priorities and what is best to help you reach your goals.

What is Best For YOU

A financial planner's goal is to determine or discover your needs and priorities. It is not to push or force you into a savings plan or investment plan that you are not comfortable with or doesn't align with your priorities.

Not everything works for everyone. I have one client who was a retired medical professional who let me know that she refused to invest any money into a few specific drug companies that tested their products on psychiatric patients. While this is a fairly extreme example, it is important to realize that you can make sure you align your investments with your personal priorities and values. That client was able to invest in mutual funds that did not include the companies she wanted to stay away from.

Chapter 10: Marguerita Cheng

The way I work with clients is to guide them. I give as much information as possible and ask a lot of questions. I am able to give advice but never push people one way or the other. They need to fully understand and commit to their priorities and goals in order to commit to reaching them.

I get mainly two types of clients who come to me. One is the people who are new to investing and making these decisions alone. For example, a widow, someone new to the workforce, or a divorcee. The idea of budgets, planning, and investing is overwhelming and they come to me because I was referred to them. The other is the type of people who have done a lot of due diligence and research and maybe have even worked with another financial planner previously, but who they felt didn't understand them. This group tends to know specifically what they do or do not want, and crave a real connection and feeling of understanding and empathy from their planner.

Just remember, not all research you find online or even hear from other financial planners will work for you. Investing and saving is not a one-size-fits-all proposition. A good financial planner will help identify strategies that are specific to your personal and financial goals.

Personal Finance

My father once told me that you either spend your money while you're alive or someone else spends it after you die. And while morbid, it's true! My dad was definitely direct and certainly didn't want anyone to be in the dark about personal finance. When you identify your priorities and figure out what you want, financial planning helps you make those plans a reality so you can enjoy your life and spend your money while you live it.

Just don't be afraid to ask questions. Then ask more questions. And more after that. I never get offended by someone asking a million questions! It's your money and your life. Digging deeper just shows you care and want to get all of the information you can. If you don't think the person you're talking to is the right fit, don't be afraid to work with a different planner. I encourage it!

It's called **personal** finance for a reason! Money is personal. Financial planning can be intimidating, but with the right help, anyone can become financially confident and resilient and set themselves up for a bright future.

CHAPTER 11

THE DREAM JOB THAT WASN'T

By **MARISA IMPELLIZZERI**

There I was, boarding my one-way direct flight from Dulles International to LAX. My dreams had come true; I made them come true. In two days, I'd be officially starting my new job as a Brand Strategist at one of the most well-known advertising agencies in the country, in the city of dreamers: Los Angeles, California. My journey to arrive here was not an easy or direct path whatsoever. It involved studying for two years among the elite at the top-ranked graduate program in the country for advertising - VCU Brandcenter - and upon presenting my final thesis, the discovery of my first gray hair. Then I relocated across the East coast to various ad agency gigs and tolerated each one's emotionally abusive supervisors, and tested the waters in alternate roles within the agency to confirm Strategist (sometimes referred to as Planner) was 100% indeed where I belonged. This all compounded with my corporate-minded parents not having one clue what I actually do. "Why don't you get an MBA?" They'd question, saying, "Be more flexible, don't narrow yourself." I'd roll my eyes and tell them that they just don't understand my creative unconventional industry while hiding my fear they could be right. Despite all this, I was going to work in exactly the role I wanted, at the agency I wanted, and in exactly the city I wanted to live in. Violet's character from the movie Coyote Ugly saying her cheesy line rang in my ear, "What are you gonna do now that you've realized all your dreams have come true?"

That's the thing about dreams; they never turn out how you expect. Not even F'ing close.

Fast forward a year into the "dream" gig, I find myself wrongfully accused of disrespecting hierarchy by my supervisor, getting the stink eye from my creative team when they passed me in the hall, and to my surprise, being removed from the weekly team meeting invitation by my snake-like account guy. As an honors International Baccalaureate, "A" student, scholarship winning, never-in-trouble, always-does-the-right-thing person, I had never felt so misunderstood in my entire life.

This is the story of a wide-eyed big dreamer from a small town in Kentucky learning the hard way that strong work ethics and, as my Mamma said, "always be kind and respectful" is not the complete ingredient list for a recipe of success. Actually, without said key ingredient, out of your metaphorical career oven will come a dish that tastes like dog sh*t.

Now, before you jump to conclusions that my story is the tired cliche of the young country bumpkin moving to a big city, let me confirm it's only half that. I was no stranger to international metropolitan city living prior to the move, having resided in Washington D.C, Dallas, the O.C., Doha Qatar, and even LA once before to attend USC. What I was a stranger to was the devious, deceitful, and egomaniacal qualities of the advertising industry.

My assigned supervisor was a quick-talking young lady not much older than me, with hurried-anxious energy, the kind that you never quite felt like you had her full attention. She was smart and experienced, I'll give her that, but fostering subordinates was 100% not a

Chapter 11: **Marisa Impellizzeri**

natural talent of hers. Micro-lesson here: Just because someone is assigned as your boss or even a few rungs above you, it does NOT qualify them whatsoever to manage people. This may be obvious to some, but I was raised with the philosophy that your boss is more experienced, thus smarter than you, therefore whatever they say or do is right. I'll just throw down a big fat naive card for this one.

Employees are often promoted to management positions with absolutely zero leadership training. I learned this is a massive problem in not just my industry but all of them, one that is going unexamined and spreading like Covid-19 before we identified the virus (too soon?). There are many essential and complex skills required of managers, such as how to delegate work, give constructive criticism, design a growth plan for each employee, inspire and empower teams, discuss promotions, and more. To put it in context, Harvard Business School's online management training program consists of 45 hours of material delivered over an eight-week period. I guess some companies think this amount of learning will just be acquired via osmosis upon day one of being promoted.

So, there I was: the eager, admittedly naive, people pleaser (the unfortunately common societal effect of most women) with the completely one-sided philosophy of "yes, sir" or "you're right, ma'am" for any authoritative figure and an entirely ill-prepared manager. I'll take you to when all things started going downhill. I was given my first big strategy assignment, to craft and present the creative brief for a decent size project on our account. My creative team and I were sitting in our "war room" concepting after my presentation. It was well past the end of the day, and I was unsure of the protocol as to whether the strategist typically joined the creatives in their concepting. My boss advised me that the creative director had it covered and to do whatever felt right. I asked the creative director if he was good, he gave me a nod yes, and I packed up my laptop to head home.

You can imagine my shock the following day during round one of the internal creative concept review that the associate creative director (ACD) howled in a tantrum-like fashion, "We got NO HELP!" directed at me. It was convenient that this was his response to my boss's constructive criticism that the concept "missed the mark." I apologized out of confusion with my knee-jerk reaction that I was wrong if a superior said so.

Shortly after, I found myself in a water cooler conversation with junior creatives explaining to me how they wished they were looped into the process earlier and wondering why strategists always work in silos rather than collaborating with the creatives early on in the process. Sounding like a reasonable request and my wrist being freshly slapped, I took it upon myself to right this wrong. The next strategy assignment I was given, I sent the junior creative team Slack messages that another quick turnaround project would be coming. My forward-thinking seemed appreciated by the worker bees, but not as much by the ACD. Remember how he complained he received no help on the last project? Yeah, it was not long after my message to the creatives that the ACD fired off a curt message instructing me to "NEVER talk to his creatives. [I] should only talk to him." This left me perplexed. It was clearly an unnecessary overreaction to misreading my proactive gesture as a power move (a sign of insecurity), not to mention an inappropriate reference to his junior talent as possessions. Was this really happening?

Chapter 11: **Marisa Impellizzeri**

It became like a domino effect. Before I could even wrap my head around what had happened, my phone rang. It was my boss requesting I meet her in the Strategy Director's office immediately. "You gave the junior team an assignment before talking with the ACD? Woof. That's pretty bad," she told me.

"No, I just gave them a heads up that a quick-turn assignment was coming down the pipeline as a courtesy. I had no bad intentions. Why was that wrong?" I found myself teary-eyed with a lump in my throat. What was happening? She only shook her head and said that it was really a bad idea. "I'll go apologize to him, I'm sorry, I was trying to help," I pleaded. She came back with, "Don't do that. You'll make a bigger deal out of it by doing that." Has this not already escalated past the normal bar?

My boss was now under the impression that I pulled a hierarchy play against the ACD, the one who complained that he got no help after my creative briefing. How did I find myself in this nightmare?

The thing I didn't realize about the advertising industry is it's a group of cliques in a middle school cafeteria and I swiftly became their target. Do you know that feeling when you walk into a room and your presence promptly triggers silence? That awkwardness became my new normal in any conversation with a team member. It spiraled so terribly. My boss abandoned the account (and me), asking to be transferred to a different client. With no supervisor given to me in the interim, I felt lost as to what to do next and asked my account guy how I could help him. He dismissed me as much with his eyes as he did with his words. I suggested that I would just relocate to the "war room" to be present if anyone else needed help. "No one really uses that anymore," he brushed me off. Even my Strategy Director seemed to be in on this ex-communication. When I told her of the account guy's dismissive tone and blatant lie about the war room, she replied, "No one wants to be asked how they can be helped." What a fool I was.

I can't quite remember the chain of events, but somewhat close to the timing of my entry into the upside-down advertising world, I had an epiphany. It was late afternoon and I was working at my desk on one of my typical assignments for the account. The client was a very well-known convenience store that sold a seasonally rotating menu of hot foods and those needed regular point of purchase ads. I was wracking my brain on how to convince a customer to buy the latest variety of chicken wings in their hot section. It suddenly dawned on me that I was actually using my master's degree to strategically manipulate less affluent shoppers of this national chain of convenience stores to buy and eat this crap. I was in a moral dilemma.

The onset of a moral complex with what I thought was my dream job became quite the mental pickle. Reflecting on this moment in my career journey and personal growth, I'm consoled by HBO's hit show Succession's interpretation of this very same conflict. Fumbling cousin Greg is shadowing his self-designated mentor and tormentor, Tom, on the first day of his new job of Head of News for Waystar. At first, it seems like a successful promotion, but it becomes clear Tom's excitement is not shared wholeheartedly by Greg. To Tom's inquiry as to what's wrong, Greg replies, "I mean, it's ATN, I don't know, it's kinda against my principles. I'm against racism and, like, don't lie." Tom laughs and says, "Come on! I'm against racism. *Everyone* is against racism. Greg, this is not f'ing Charles Dickens's world. You don't go

Chapter 11: **Marisa Impellizzeri**

around talking about principles. We're all trying to do the right thing. Come on man! Man the f*** up."

What struck me the most was Tom's reaction to Greg's brave admission of this seemingly good opportunity being against his values. How immature to express one's boundaries in the business world. "Grow up!" Tom declares with annoyance. Was this the reality of the modern business environment? Was I so blind or sheltered to not see this? Comparing Greg's moral complex to mine in tandem with the exaggerated misunderstanding spreading like wildfire to convince an entire team to rally against me with lies and omission became a hard pill to swallow. My world was shaken.

But not for long. With every failure, disappointment, and heartbreak there is a lesson. Needless to say, that "dream job" didn't last. Believe it or not, I am still working in advertising. I went on to lead strategy at a nimble social and digital agency just a block down the street. It's funny how small the ad world is. My performance at my new job was so impressive that my boss recruited me to be the VP of Strategy at his start-up agency in Venice Beach, where I am now. How did I make the leap from ground-shaking emotional abuse and moral complex to my comfortable title? The lesson is conviction.

What I realized is I had the tools and foundation to do great things, but what I never quite acquired was **the conviction that I was capable** of using those tools for great things. The conviction that my experience and point of view are valid, often more valid than that of my superiors. And I need to protect that conviction with my whole being. The sad reality is there always will be people who try to take you down or take advantage of your feminine niceties for their greed because to them, getting ahead is greater than everything. My values to lead with kindness will always guide me. Projecting my values allowed other people to come forth, too, they attracted them to me and me to them. I found my tribe. The truth is there is a tribe for everyone. Believe you deserve it and are wholly capable and go out and kick ass!

CHAPTER 12

HOW TO TURN LIFE'S CHALLENGES INTO GIFTS: A JOURNEY FROM CANCER SURVIVOR TO CEO

By **MICHELLE MEKKY**

When I was starting high school, it was difficult for me to envision myself as a confident adult with a fulfilling career, let alone as the founder and president of a thriving public relations agency. Like so many teens, I was plagued with insecurities and a lack of direction during those formative years. I was the child of immigrants who worked hard but struggled to support our family. I didn't have the designer clothes so many kids were wearing, and my mouthful of braces and uncontrollably curly hair only contributed to my lack of confidence.

But I did have two things going for me which made all the difference:
1. I was a hard worker and incredibly driven to succeed - I knew I could be a leader and make a difference.
2. I had some inspiring English teachers at Niles West High School in Skokie, Illinois, who encouraged me to join the school newspaper and audition for a TV news program, and then I was selected as the anchor!

That's when things started to change for me. It still took me many years to find my confidence, but high school journalism gave me a purpose and helped me realize my passion for storytelling, starting me on a path that would eventually lead to my life's work.

After high school, I was fortunate to attend Northwestern University, where I got my bachelor's and master's degrees from the Medill School of Journalism. My Northwestern years expanded my horizons and led to opportunities I could never have imagined just a few years before. But they were also a time of back-breaking work, through challenging classes and the four jobs I worked to help support myself. I believe this period gave me a resiliency that would serve me well working long hours as I launched and continued to advance my career.

I jumped right into the news business after college, spending over a decade as a senior producer and news writer for FoxTV in Chicago. These years were full of long, hard hours. I had my son and daughter during this time and came to realize that the grueling schedule did not allow me to devote enough time to being a new mom. I had gotten to know many of the PR professionals who booked their clients on our program, and I admired the role they played in getting stories out to the public. With my journalism background and insider media knowledge and connections, I felt that I could excel in public relations.

So, I made the transition to PR and marketing. I spent over 10 years at agencies in Chicago, where I enjoyed the more consistent schedule (although still long hours) and achieving top-tier media coverage for the clients I managed, including some major national brands.

Chapter 12: **Michelle Mekky**

But this exciting time came to a crashing halt in 2015. I was at a checkup, probably in a hurry to get to my next meeting when my doctor informed me that something was very wrong. It turned out to be ovarian cancer. These were terrifying words to hear. But I was one of the lucky few. My cancer was found early, and I was able to have surgery and eventually make a full recovery.

Still, it seemed like an eternity before I started feeling like myself again. I'm so grateful to have been surrounded by the love of my husband, mom, and other family and friends during that scary time in my life. And, of course, I'm thankful every single day for my health. I know many are not as fortunate.

I returned to work, but with a new outlook and a promise that I would make every day count. I started having serious conversations with myself about what that really meant. This led to the realization that having my own business might be my destiny.

Ironically, in summer 2016, as I was beginning to consider what this possibility could look like, I lost my job. The company made a change and it was traumatic, even though it turned out to be the best thing for me in the long-term. I spent the first several days at home pondering my next steps. And then I had a life-changing conversation with a close friend and mentor. She asked, "What are you waiting for? You know you can do this." And she did more than make a suggestion. She put up the capital I needed to launch my dream. And just like that, Mekky Media Relations Inc., my boutique PR firm, was born.

Powerful Publicity - On My Terms

Armed with a company name, I sat down in my dining room and started emailing my contacts. The support I received gave me the confidence to push forward into this new and unfamiliar territory. I quickly landed my first client. From there, things took off. And they haven't slowed since.

Starting Mekky Media has been an exciting, and sometimes terrifying roller coaster ride. The hours were grueling for the first couple of years and the nights were sleepless. My kids were entering their teens, and I was constantly feeling guilty that I couldn't spend more time with them. Thankfully, my supportive husband jumped right in and I started to build a team I could trust.

Mekky Media experienced an explosion of growth during our fast-paced launch, with a diverse roster of clients signing on. Businesses continue to seek us out four years later. Even during the height of the COVID-19 pandemic, we took on new projects as clients turned to us to communicate how they were pivoting to meet the needs of their communities.

I've also grown my team, with approximately 10 PR professionals now part of the agency. We focus on PR strategy and media relations, media training, event promotion, social media strategy, and influencer outreach. Our clients have ranged from startups to established businesses, including Abt Electronics, Francesca's Restaurant Group, Impact XM, TCS Education System, TimeZoneOne, Wealth Management Group, and West Edge Design (our first Los Angeles client!). In addition, I've been proud to represent some of Chicago's top nonprofits, including the Center for Enriched Living, Chicago Lights, Chicago Scholars, Devices 4 the Disabled, IES Abroad, the Muslim American Leadership Alliance, and Susan G. Komen Chicago. My work as a spokesperson for the National Ovarian Cancer Coalition has also been so rewarding.

Chapter 12: **Michelle Mekky**

Mekky Media has helped these and many other clients tell their stories through millions of media impressions in online, print, and broadcast outlets in Chicago and nationally. We've been honored many times over for these results, including the 2020 and 2018 Bronze Stevie Awards for PR Agency of the Year and Entrepreneur of the Year. I was also named a Crain's Chicago Business Notable Entrepreneur, an honor that blew me away, considering how I've admired Crain's honorees over the years.

It's been a long and sometimes arduous journey to get to this point in my career and in the life of Mekky Media, but it's so worth it when I consider the contributions we make to organizations I deeply respect, the team I'm honored to collaborate with every day, and the rewarding, creative work we do together.

Tips for Women Leaders or Those Who Aspire to Get There

From my teachers at Niles West to media and PR pros to my mentor who made Mekky Media a reality, I have been shaped and guided by some incredible women. They have helped me develop the skills I required, lifted me up when I needed it most, and given me opportunities for which I am forever grateful. I'm a believer in mentorship and passing along the knowledge and experience I've gained from these generous individuals.

Here are some of the tips and advice which has been most important and helpful in my journey, as well as some of the hard lessons I've learned along the way:

Landing the client, job, employee, or project of your dreams: Just go for it!

We all have bold aspirations that require extreme confidence to pursue. Sometimes "going for it" can feel like jumping off a cliff. But we all know that nothing great comes from playing it safe. Many times, I have had to dig deep to find my nerve as a female entrepreneur. Has it always worked out? No. But often, it has - and those experiences have taken my business to the next level. My failures have also taught me a lot, and I don't regret them. Here's what I've learned about taking risks:

1. **Level the playing field:**
   It doesn't matter what someone's title is or what kind of car they drive, they are probably like you in more ways than you know. And they might need what you have to offer. So, don't get so intimidated that you avoid putting yourself out there.
2. **Name your dream:**
   Start by figuring out what your dream is and naming it, then get specific about your motivations and aspirations. This will help you manifest your desires and hold yourself accountable. You'll achieve more once you have this clarity.
3. **Trust your gut:**
   Identifying my dream clients or employees has often been based on gut feelings. When it comes to working with people, this is a tried and true barometer that you should lean into. Take the facts and figures and how something looks on paper into account as well, but don't discount your gut.
4. **Be authentic:** See the next tip!

Chapter 12: **Michelle Mekky**

Stay authentic and why it matters

When launching a business or relationship, it's tempting to say yes to everything. You're in a growth mindset and to grow, we have to give the people what they want, right? The problem is that some people will take advantage of a yes-yes attitude, which means you and/or your team will suffer. So, be forthcoming from the start about what you can and cannot provide. When you're transparent, the right relationships will reveal themselves to you. Authenticity also means that I try to only work with people I truly believe in. I'm incredibly fortunate to be able to choose to promote clients who have missions I can wholeheartedly get behind.

Another aspect of authenticity is leading and living with vulnerability. We can sometimes feel like we're drowning in a social media sea of fake images, attitudes, and lives. This contributes to the unrealistic aspirations many of us have for ourselves. Remaining authentic in life and online is a core value of mine - and of my business. I admit I'm not perfect, that I don't have all the answers, and that I continue to experience failure. I try to show the less glamorous aspects of my life in addition to the fun in order to show myself realistically and authentically.

Learn from your mistakes

For an entrepreneur, mistakes can be personally and professionally transformative. As a perfectionist, I have found this hard to accept. The key is to recognize that occasional failure is inevitable and be open to the possibilities it can present. Here are three mistakes I don't regret making:

1. **I didn't have enough confidence.**
   When I took the leap to become a business owner, I suffered from "impostor syndrome." I worried people would find out I didn't have what it takes. That was a mistake, but moving forward in spite of it gave me strength and got me where I am today. It also gave me the ability to support and mentor others who are taking risks to achieve their dreams.
2. **I sacrificed my family for work.**
   When you're an entrepreneur, the demands never end. But I regret being a workaholic and losing precious time with my family. The positive side is this forced me to confront the work/life imbalance in my life. I'm now better at establishing boundaries and more intentional in how I spend my time.
3. **I got sucked into gossip.**
   When I was younger and gossip was insidious in the newsroom, it felt impossible to avoid it. Had I been more secure with myself, I could have risen above it. But being young and hungry, I wanted to make a good impression on my colleagues. This ended up inhibiting my ability to trust others. In the end, though, this experience provided the insight to seek out trustworthy women to surround myself with, which is now a priority for me.

Mistakes and failures are a part of life and business. The key is learning from them and moving forward as a stronger, better person and business owner.

Bonus tip: How to get publicity for your company

Many businesses feel they must pay for advertising to promote themselves in a way that improves their bottom line. However, an effective PR campaign can also have a positive impact at a lower cost.

Chapter 12: **Michelle Mekky**

That's why more organizations are turning to PR, especially as marketing and advertising budgets are shrinking.

Here's a quick cheat sheet to help you tell your story:

1. **Make a list of why you're special.**
   Write at least five bullet points that identify your most important messaging. Do you have a unique service? Is there a sentimental angle or are you helping a community that's in need? What's your history? What sets you apart from the competition?
2. **Communicate consistently.**
   Keep your messaging at the forefront of all communications. Spread it far and wide, whether in media pitches, social media posts, or presentations.
3. **Understand the media.**
   It can be tough to get media attention if you don't have a publicist with media expertise and connections, but you should be able to have some success getting your story out there if you devote time to research. Remember that people in the media get hundreds of pitches a day. You won't get a response if you aren't targeting the appropriate outlets and contacts.
4. **Harness the power of social media.**
   In addition to pitching traditional media, use social media to tell your story. Find the platforms that work best for your business and post engaging content on a regular basis. If necessary, take a class about how to write for social media and create compelling images and videos. This medium is important and it's worth a little extra investment.

I hope these tips are helpful to people in various stages of their career journeys. Women are not always supportive of each other, and I think we should all work to change this dynamic whenever we encounter it. I believe it's incredibly important to support and celebrate each other and to share our knowledge.

I've had a lot of odds stacked against me at various points in my life - insecurities as a teen and into adulthood, cancer, job loss, and more. It was not a likely path toward starting a successful business. But I have consistently found that confidence, hard work, and passion can overcome many challenges, as can surrounding yourself with the right people.

CHAPTER 13

IRON SHARPENING IRON

By **RACQUEL RIVERA**

It can be terrifying to start over.

Or at least it feels like starting over. As a results-driven, ambitious woman, I didn't have to look too hard to find my passions but figuring out how to turn those into a long-lasting and satisfying career was less obvious.

Despite personal and health struggles, I never lost my drive to succeed. Despite doubts and obstacles life threw in my way, I made the conscious choice to pivot my career at 40 years old - and I wish I would have taken more risks and done it much sooner.

Before pivoting into real estate, I spent my twenties and thirties in other creative and demanding careers. I worked with venture capitalists, connecting them with startups in the entertainment industry, as an executive assistant for Kathleen Wirt at her recording studio for eight years, worked at a talent management company, and ran the special events division of a restaurant group.

The combination of creativity and business with a dash of entrepreneurship calls to me. That's why real estate ended up being the perfect choice. It requires tenacity, diligence, patience, perseverance, creative marketing, and the ability to truly connect with people.

But it was not an easy path and I want to encourage people, especially women, to take risks and follow their dreams. I actually fell into real estate; I met a beautiful woman, Bonnie Burke, who was a real estate broker in the Pacific Palisades while I worked at Nordstroms part-time because I was in school. She said I would be really great at real estate and helped me get my license. I owe the start of my real estate career to her. I was with her boutique brokerage for a short stint, but left because I lived in Laurel Canyon and her office was in the Pacific Palisades and I was still in school, so I wasn't ready to make the commitment.

I wish I'd done it sooner. A couple years after I'd gotten my real estate license, I still procrastinated jumping into real estate 100% because I was nervous about leaving a stable job with benefits for the potentially unknown world of real estate. At the time, my real estate license was with a brokerage that didn't have any crazy fees and I was working in the hospitality industry. I met so many people and loved being social, plus I was still getting several real estate leads. I partnered up with a gentleman at the agency I was with and just handed off leads to him left and right, making referral fees instead of bonafide commissions. I knew I had to jump in, despite the fear. Because at some point, the fear of not every trying overtook my desire to stay safe.

And despite people telling me I couldn't or shouldn't make such a big change, despite health challenges and a bad relationship, I persevered. Not that it's been simple or easy or without bumps in the road, of course.

Chapter 13: **Racquel Rivera**

What I've learned most in my journey has been to not listen to people telling you that you can't do something and that with big risks come great rewards.

You Don't Have To Do It Alone

I was stuck in an "I have to do it all myself!" mentality. This isn't true! Everything in life is a collaboration and work should be no different. Even though real estate is an incredibly entrepreneurial career, it does not have to be a lonely or singular one.

In my early years of real estate, I was with a different non-dues brokerage that really didn't offer much in terms of training or support or even partnership. One of my first sales was an investment property in Woodland Hills. It took about two months for me to locate the property, show it, negotiate, and close the deal. I **could** do it all but recognized that there were areas I needed help with.

I'm very good at working with people, communication skills, resourcefulness, and negotiating, but I struggled more with contracts and some of the more technical details.

I realized I was actually missing out on opportunities because there was a learning curve and I was just trying to do everything myself.

Partnering with someone changed my perspective and provided needed support, learning, and development. I would absolutely encourage anyone starting in real estate to look for either an agency or a team that provides training and ongoing development. Don't just jump into the deep end and hope you can figure it out as you go along. Why make it harder on yourself? There isn't some special prize for struggling!

Part of being a good business person is knowing your strengths and weaknesses. By partnering with an individual or a team with complementary skills, the entire team is stronger than if any of you were alone.

For me, I choose to work with strong women I can learn from and support.

To find a partner, the first thing I did was ask for recommendations from others. I also researched agencies I thought might be a good fit for me and specifically researched the women working at those agencies.

In one case, I found a woman through my research and one of my friends knew her and introduced us. While the partnership didn't last long, I learned a lot! Sometimes the lessons you learn are about what you do **not** want or need, instead of about positive things. This partnership taught me that I needed to be confident and stand up for myself to get what I deserve, and I also learned that I had to ask for what I want. No one is going to just give you things for free. You have to ask for them, sometimes just take them, and yes, it can occasionally ruffle feathers. But you are your own best advocate and are the only one who will always have your own best interests at heart.

Life Gets In The Way Sometimes

Having a passion and finding your path doesn't suddenly make life easy. We all have our battles and you never know what someone is facing or dealing with behind closed doors. This is one reason why

Chapter 13: **Racquel Rivera**

I feel compassion and empathy are among the most important tools when working with others.

It seemed like I was being hit from all sides. I had my own family members doubting my decision to pivot into real estate, I felt like my age might be a barrier, my car broke down, I was dipping into my savings, and then I got sick. I felt completely stuck. Now, being on the other side of the worst of those struggles, I know that my faith in God and faith in myself are what got me through.

Despite my symptoms, I was just trying to stay afloat and focus on work. I thought I had cancer. I was in pain, very sick, and had extreme issues with low energy. It was affecting my work, even though I kept forcing myself to work despite pain. I went to multiple doctors, and while kind and knowledgeable, they couldn't figure out what was wrong with me.

One day, my bloodwork came back and my hemoglobin level was at 5 g/dL (average for women is 12.1 to 15.1 g/dL or 121 to 151 g/L). I was sick, hemorrhaging, and anemic. I had two blood transfusions in six months and for an entire year, I was in the doctor's office every Monday. Eventually, a specialist figured out what was happening and she took care of everything.

Even while sick, I was pushing through to go to work. I was building my pipeline and wanted to be successful despite the odds being stacked against me. I was hoping the illness wouldn't last forever and I had to keep pushing through any fear and physical hindrances. Unfortunately, despite my tenacity, my sickness took a toll on my work performance (and mental faculties), and I was let go of the group I was part of. I will never forget when the office manager suggested that I should be a real estate transaction coordinator! I don't blame her; in fact, I know she wanted to see me succeed. But deep down inside, I knew I would never quit and settle. Not long after I was let go, I was physically healed. I was so sad that I was let go of this group and felt like a total failure.

I soon met a wonderful woman named Jennifer Lowe at Moonshadows restaurant in Malibu. She was a mortgage broker and an investor at a brokerage. She made a phone call and brought me in for an interview, then I was officially with Pacific Union International. The company was eventually purchased by Compass, where I still work.

In the end, I am able to be grateful it happened but extremely glad it's over! I pushed past the judgment of friends and family, and especially from colleagues who didn't understand my illness.

I learned a lot about myself - my perseverance, drive, and what I am capable of. I no longer feel guilty for wanting to succeed and know I'm smart and can thrive in this business. Being a woman, it can feel like a delicate line between confidence and off-putting arrogance and I no longer care about that line. I have learned it's okay to be confident and proud of myself and my work.

Moving Forward with Confidence

After a year of working at Compass, I partnered with a strong, beautiful woman - heaven-sent actually - Jennifer Petsu. I'd built a big pipeline and was working with Jennifer on her deals, but my own deals were not panning out. I decided to give myself a time limit that if nothing came through by the end of the year, I would reassess and pivot once again to a new career.

Chapter 13: **Racquel Rivera**

A week later, a luxury lease came through and it snowballed. Suddenly, several deals in a row were coming to completion after months and months of work. I gained more confidence in my work and even got some out of state referrals.

I decided to invest in myself and my own self-care and finally learned to stop feeling guilty for prioritizing myself and my needs or for being successful.

I am looking forward to more fun projects in the future, such as starting a YouTube channel and a podcast and sharing more about women in real estate with the world.

Fighting through personal, health, and work challenges help you identify what is truly important and worth fighting for. It doesn't matter if others don't believe in you; you have to believe in yourself and push and fight to succeed despite all opposition.

CHAPTER 14

IMPLEMENTING VALUE-BASED CARE FOR CANCER PATIENTS

By **RANI KHETARPAL**

The path that led me to be in the field I am was, like most journeys, not straightforward. In fact, this particular field and area of expertise did not even exist a decade ago. After a brief exploration of the field of broadcast journalism, I was encouraged to pursue a field in medicine. Although the medical field is vast, the "medical field" translated to "medical doctor" for me, nothing more and nothing less. I gave it a shot, but after my first couple of years in college, I realized it wasn't my calling. So, I switched to business. Armed with a business degree and a lot of science classes I didn't want to waste, I attended a career fair where pharmaceutical manufacturers were recruiting. And thus, my journey began. Fast-forward a couple of decades and here I am, an entrepreneur, healthcare executive, wife, and mom with an amazing family.

My foray into oncology happened as a side effect of my desire to "be the best" - a phrase that was branded into me by mom. Oncology at the time was considered the top echelon in pharmaceuticals - it was prestigious, it paid the best out of all specialties, and had the greatest potential for professional growth and leadership opportunities. It was in a world of its own and I wanted to be in it. And so, I did. Little did I realize that it would become a passion for me that extends far beyond professional achievements. I find myself now in the center of a movement that is changing the way cancer care is delivered. It is a new frontier that not only fuels my entrepreneurial spirit, it is literally giving me opportunities to make a difference at a much broader level that has a domino effect on individual patients. There is little known outside of those who are entrenched in this world about what this change, what it entails, and how it is happening. My personal story is intertwined with the knowledge I share around this new way of oncology care. I wish I had known then what I know now but this is all happening in real-time. I am grateful that my journey has led me to be a part of this transformation in healthcare, and specifically now for oncology. A much-needed change for a disease that changes lives with three small words: "You have cancer."

In an unfortunate truth, we all know someone who has been affected by cancer. Whether it was you, a friend, or a family member, the big C does not discriminate. My maternal grandmother died of breast cancer in the summer of 2018. My grandfather also passed away from cancer - years before when I was very young and didn't really understand what cancer was. Now, as an executive at an organization dedicated to supporting the movement toward value-based care in oncology, I am heavily involved in the strategy to make cancer care more affordable, more easily understood, and how to best educate all those involved on what drives the value equation in oncology, ultimately leading to informed decisions by providers and patients.

Four years ago, my grandmother was diagnosed with metastatic breast cancer. Metastatic is the medical term meaning that the cancer had spread from the original site of the tumor to other organs in her body. Even though I worked in various aspects of oncology for many years, and despite my brother and sister-in-law being physicians, the three of us were not involved in my grandmother's care or treatment. Instead, another family member was in charge of her care. Unfortunately, how my grandmother was treated at the end of her life was appalling. In the end, she passed away in the ICU after suffering unimaginable pain.

Unfortunately, my story is far from the exception and this experience is all too common in the medical field. Many times, it's the family members who are being asked to make decisions, along with the patient. Even with a greater push to educate and support decision-making throughout the patient journey, the family of the cancer patient is overwhelmed, stressed out, extremely emotional, and they are being asked to make medical decisions they do not fully understand.

Many organizations, including the one I currently work for, have been working toward developing delivery models, products, and solutions that support value-based care (VBC), a concept to combat this experience of uninformed decision-making, among other things, into oncology. VBC is essentially a healthcare delivery model in which healthcare providers, including hospitals, are paid based on outcomes that are adjudicated on the balance of quality and cost of care. In oncology, VBC also aims to provide patients and family/caregivers a transparent process and an informed journey when dealing with treatment, including treatment plans, end of life care options, detailed explanations and education throughout the process, and the ability to keep better track of the patient's journey.

Value-based care has been implemented in other medical fields, but because cancer care is so complex and has so many facets beyond just the initial diagnosis, it has been left alone until just a few years ago. Over the last 5-7 years, the oncology community has invested heavily in finding ways to improve the costs of cancer care without sacrificing the quality of care. This problem is far from being solved, but there has been forward movement and strides have been made to improve the system. The development of innovative payment models for both government and private payers, and the development of products and solutions to support the providers to achieve success in these models has led to a better understanding of how to succeed in balancing this complex equation.

The most important message here is that the way cancer care has been delivered is changing. It is imperative that everyone who needs to be is informed on the rapid evolution of cancer care and how it affects decisions being made by providers, patients, and payers, and further, how those three categories must work together to ultimately ensure the patient gets the best care possible.

The Business of Oncology

Traditionally, cancer care has been a fee-for-service payment model. A patient goes to the doctor, gets their treatment and care, and then the doctor bills the insurance company for everything. The insurance company then approves or denies the coverage and pays what they feel is best, and the patient either pays their co-pay and any remaining balance as dictated by their insurance plan.

This "fee-for-service" payment model is still in place now, but as healthcare is transforming, the insurance companies (payers) are starting to realize that this is an expensive model with basically no checks and balances in place. Furthermore, the payer is typically not involved directly in the care of the patient, but can deny payments if they deem something to be unnecessary, even if a doctor says it is necessary for the patient.

Doctors in this model have the freedom to prescribe drugs and treatment options as they see fit, but the insurance companies also have the ability to deny a particular drug. And as more and more expensive options become available, this becomes an issue for both the doctor and the patients. This is where VBC can be helpful. With a VBC model in place, we can look at more cost-effective treatments (cost) without compromising the patient's care and treatment plan (quality). Thus, the benefit to the triad - patient, provider, payer - is realized. That is the intent of VBC.

The concept of value-based care took shape in the mid-1990s and was discussed further in the early 2000s. Under Obama's Affordable Care Act, it became a reality. The Center for Medicare and Medicaid Innovation (CMMI) began pushing and deploying alternative payment models (APMs), which is the driver behind value-based care.

APMs really started with more controllable physiologies, such as joints and cardiology treatments. It started as being able to "bundle" payments - a set price for patients being treated for a particular condition or requiring a certain procedure. The concept is simple in theory - if the actual cost of care for that bundle is higher than the set amount, then the provider loses money; if the actual cost of care is lower, the provider makes money. This model is considered a "risk" model, as the provider is at risk of losing money if the cost of care exceeds the bundle. Therefore, they are incentivized to make conscious decisions around treatments and ensure the provider is accountable for the care they provide. Sounds good, right? It is, in theory. This is complex to execute and requires a high level of resource investment on the part of the provider. But if successful, the incentives are high.

However, the bundled payment model doesn't easily work for oncology. Cancer has proven to be very complex and unpredictable to be part of the bundled payment movement, So, for a very long time, cancer care was left to exist in the traditional fee-for-service model. Oncology is always rapidly evolving in treatments and treatment modalities, and the cancer itself is not always easy to predict in its behavior. Other factors that complicate this even further include the type of cancer being treated, how far it has progressed, and if the cancer has spread. In addition, there is a constant stream of new and experimental medications, clinical trials, patient care pathways, and more. Clinical trials, especially, are extremely important in oncology, as a patient's prognosis may actually rely on drugs that are not publicly available yet, but could be accessible through trials. All of these factors play into a care delivery system that is far more complex that one can possibly imagine.

Another reason why cancer care has been left untouched is the fact that cancer is such an emotional topic for so many. Arguably, the three most dreaded words one can hear are "You have cancer." But it is a disservice to stay away from it, not only because it is so very expensive - indeed, one of the highest costs in the entire healthcare system - but also because patients deserve to have the best treatment possible. So, the question becomes: How can we tackle cancer care delivery in a way that values the patient's needs and diagnoses, without always going for the most expensive option, and create more informed decision-making throughout their cancer care journey?

Value-Based Care

In a value-based care payment model, our aim is to give the patient better care but lowering the costs and continuing to improve the quality of treatments, while advocating for more informed patients.

Chapter 14: **Rani Khetarpal**

In cancer there, there are three highest-cost controllable expenses:
- Drugs/Treatment
- ER/Hospitalization
- End of life care

Drugs/Treatment

You may be surprised to learn that in the cost of cancer care, a full 50% of the cost, if not more, is due to drug costs alone. The popular thought is that drug spend cannot be controlled in cancer care, due to the various options and treatment levels. However, as recently published in the peer-reviewed Journal of Oncology Practice, drugs can be "controllable expense" in cancer care.

There have been over 30 years of intensive ongoing research in this field. Until about 10 years ago, there was a pretty steady incline in the cost of drugs and treatments for cancer patients. Then, around seven years ago, there was a sudden drastic increase in drug and therapy costs. The exponential rise in costs had a very dramatic effect on the increase in the total cost of cancer. This was expected and, truthfully, warranted. The newer drugs have shown an ability to prolong life, eradicate some cancers, and improve quality of life, making treatment easier for the vast majority of patients. But this does not come without cost.

However, newer does not always mean better. Just because a drug or treatment is newer and/ or more expensive does not mean it is more effective for every patient. Many times, patients will see an advertisement for a new drug and they'll ask their doctor about it because they want the "latest and greatest." But the issue is that not only does the patient not know about the clinical aspects of the drug or the cost impact of the new drug, they also usually don't know or understand if the new drug is up to the "standard of care" as other drugs and treatments they'd been recommended to use. With new and novel therapies, some simply have not been proven to be up to the same standard of care as the other existing treatments.

The standard of care refers to the "gold" standard for that particular cancer or condition. Gold standard means that the risks and effects of the drug are well-known, proven, and is currently the best therapy for what it is treating. Standard of care changes as newer drugs are released, tested, and proven over time. For example, the standard of care drugs for lung cancer used to be able to be treated at a very reasonable cost, and, in fact, those treatments still work well. However, when a class of drugs known as PD1 was made available, the standard of care for lung cancer shifted, since the efficacy of these drugs was so great. And with that shift, the cost for treating lung cancer has skyrocketed. Because PD1s are now the standard of care, a doctor is now likely to prescribe that as a "first-line therapy" for a lung cancer patient, despite the extremely high cost to the payer, provider, and the patient. Until PD1s are available in a generic or biosimilar form, the cost will likely continue to stay very high. But ultimately, the cost is warranted.

This is not always the case and the important thing to remember here is that in many cases, the older treatment regimens still work and are effective. There are many factors that need to be considered in choosing a regimen, but the three main questions are: Does it work? What is the drug's toxicity (side effects)? What is the value of the treatment for the patient (quality versus cost)?

So, how do providers know how to choose a treatment that balances quality and cost? This is where clinical pathways come in. Value-based clinical pathways are evidence-based: that is, data points from various clinical studies are extracted, aggregated, and analyzed to determine what the best quality-driven treatments are for various cancers. An internationally-recognized organization, the National Comprehensive Cancer Network (NCCN), publishes a compendium of guidelines for all the different treatments available for specific cancer types. This compendium is used as one of many sources for clinical pathway companies to derive outcome-based clinical pathways, which are used as a resource in APMs and other value-based care initiatives.

ER/Hospitalization

The second major controllable expense is emergency room visits and being admitted to a hospital.

Here is the reality: If a patient is on active chemotherapy treatment, they will have side effects. Some are more severe than others, but 60-70% of all emergency room visits for chemo side effects are PREVENTABLE.

As soon as a patient walks into the emergency room, the average cost for that ER visit is $4500-6500. If they are admitted to the hospital, the cost goes way up. And no matter what side effect you have, if you are on chemo, there is a greater than 60% chance you will be admitted "just in case." In the traditional fee-for-service payment models, the idea is that if anything goes wrong, send people to the hospital.

I said that the majority of these ER visits are preventable, but how can you prevent them?

Well, in value-based care, with the focus on the value to and for the patient, we have seen that instituting programs that provide a consistent and standardized way of handling the inflow of side effect complaints, such as standardized triaging, prevents many unnecessary emergency room visits. A patient contacts the office and informs the triage nurse of their symptom(s) and/or side effect(s). The nurse then uses a standardized protocol or pathway to "triage" the patient to the appropriate site of care with the nurse's approval. This process determines if the complaint is severe enough to warrant an ER visit or require a doctor's visit, in which case the nurse would schedule an appointment with the doctor instead of sending the patient to the ER. The nurse can also determine if it is a minor or expected side effect and tell the patient how they can mitigate or treat the symptom at home.

Programs like these add another level of care and oversight to the process and prevent unnecessary and expensive ER visits and hospitalizations. It often comes down to symptom management and saves the sick patient time and money. This type of program also has non-financial benefits for cancer patients. They don't have the stress of the emergency room visit, they can see their regular doctor with whom they feel more comfortable, and they have a lower risk of infection because they won't be exposed to other illnesses or infections at the hospital while they are immunocompromised from the chemo treatment.

End of Life Care

The last controllable expense is the money associated with end of life care for cancer patients. This can be one of the most difficult and emotional periods of the patient journey, especially for the family members and caregivers. But it is extremely important to talk about.

Chapter 14: **Rani Khetarpal**

Regardless of where the patient is in their cancer journey, there needs to be advanced care planning. An Advanced Care Plan (ACP) is a plan that is executed when the patient enters the period that is termed the end of life, meaning they are nearing their stage where death is imminent. The ACP needs to be discussed and decided upon early in their cancer treatment and usually involves family members and those closest to the patient. The patients care team - provider, nurse, social worker - are also involved in the discussion.

Why is this so important? My grandmother did not have an ACP. As a result, because of how rapidly her cancer progressed, she did not have a voice in how she died. Furthermore, the burden put on my family, and the emotional toll was unimaginable. There is no doubt that with an ACP, much of this could have been avoided and we would have known exactly what she wanted.

In value-based care, this stage of life is looked at not only to ensure there is dignity for the patient when this stage becomes imminent but also to ensure the patient's loved ones are involved and understand what will happen when this stage arrives. In most cases, without an ACP, the patient will defer to a family member, who 9 times out of 10, wants to keep their loved one alive as long as possible. Understandably so! How could you possibly make a decision that makes the death of your loved one a harsh reality? But countless studies have shown that there is no real benefit to trying to "save" someone once they are nearing the end of their life with cancer. The optimal approach is to keep the patient comfortable, pain-free, and allow death with dignity - not hooked up to machines with active chemo being infused into their body.

Of course, this is tricky and emotional. The family wants to keep treating the patient as long as possible and keep trying new drugs and therapies. In traditional fee-for-service care, the doctor would be more apt to go along with what the family desires, and it could unfortunately result in a less than dignified death. In value-based care, the end of life care is more intentional. The patient's care team speaks in-depth with the patient and their family and discusses their options and the consequences of these options long before the patient is reaching the end of their life. This includes types of care such as palliative care and hospice. They take the time to educate and inform the patient and their family to give the patient a chance for a more dignified end of life.

Doctors are acutely aware chemotherapy does not really do anything more for cancer patients in the last two weeks of life. In fact, many cancer patients die from the side effects of chemo at the end, because at that point it is doing more harm than good. Stopping chemotherapy in those last weeks and keeping the patient's quality of life as stable as possible is usually a better choice. This could include palliative and/or appropriate hospice care. Ideally, a patient nearing the end of life will enter into palliative care first, and only spend the appropriate number of days in hospice, as close to the end as can be predicted. The goal is to prevent the patient from having to die in the hospital.

There is no doubt that this type of care should be standard for all oncology patients regardless of value-based care models. Doctors may say they just don't have time to have these long educational discussions with patients and their families. Or doctors know that the patient's wishes and their family's wishes won't match and they don't want to get involved. But patients must be prepared and the end of life discussions are crucial to being educated and as emotionally prepared as possible for this potential outcome.

One solution to ensure hard conversations take place is to expand the role of the nurse navigator in oncology offices. A nurse navigator is a specially trained nurse or social worker who guides the patient through the clinical and emotional aspects of their cancer journey. While nurse navigators are not required across the board, in the government-run value-based care model, this role is required. There have been several studies showing the value of the nurse navigator role in both clinical and non-clinical aspects of the cancer patient's journey. Unfortunately, a navigator's time is not reimbursable in a traditional fee-for-service model and as such, many practices have yet to invest in a true navigator role. There is work being done currently to change this, though this change will take some time. Another potential solution is utilizing technology platforms that provide information and education for family members and patients. This has gained some traction over the last couple of years and it is expected to become a more common way to educate and communicate with patients. Yet another solution is to have a palliative care physician have this difficult discussion with the patient and their family. However, palliative care doctors in oncology are not commonplace or readily available, although it is gaining quite a bit of attention due to its impact on quality of care.

Bottom line: No matter how it comes about, discussing end of life care earlier in the process and honoring the patient and coming at it from a value-based care model is very important.

Bringing it All Home

Recently, a post reached me via social media. The post was for a GoFundMe request for a friend whose husband passed away that morning from cancer. He had been battling cancer for three years. He had gone into remission for some time, only to have the cancer reappear in another manner, this time spreading so aggressively they could not stop it. He went on clinical trials hoping for a miracle but in the end, he lost his battle, leaving behind his wife and three kids aged 8-12. I have another close friend who had a brain tumor over a decade ago and just celebrated her tenth year cancer-free. These two cases show that cancer doesn't discriminate; it is unpredictable, and forever changes lives. Yes, the "c" word is scary, powerful, complex, unpredictable, and emotional. I don't foresee these descriptives changing any time soon.

However, what is changing is the way we look at treating cancer. Although there is much work yet to be done to better understand what the best approach will be to deliver cancer care, one thing is for sure: there will not likely ever be a one-size-fits-all option for treating cancer. What is certain is that the work being done in value-based care allows for patients and providers to come together to make informed decisions about their care, which ultimately will result in a patient-centered approach that provides for the best patient care possible. If that allows just one person or family to have a better experience, then the effort is absolutely worth it.

CHAPTER 15

HOW HIGH IS YOUR EQ? THE CASE FOR SOCIAL EMOTIONAL INTELLIGENCE

By **RENEE LOPEZ-CANTERA**

After working in digital marketing, direct sales, and real estate industries for almost 23 years, I have looked back to try to understand what top skills or traits have helped me the most in business.

Emotional intelligence, or EQ, skills have been very important in my career. Hindsight is always 20/20 (ironic that we are publishing this book in the year 2020), but **empathy** would be my number one personal trait that has made an impact in my life. Have you considered what your top three traits might be? Have you asked yourself, a friend, mentor, or colleague to give you feedback on this topic?

Back at Tulane in my college sorority Pi Beta Phi, we had a certain ceremony celebrating the "Best of" categories. I remember being voted Most Empathetic. Little did I know that this one skill would be huge in my future career and even more so in my personal life. Often, understanding the motives of others by cognitively putting myself in their shoes has been the difference between closing versus losing deals.

Another trait which has propelled me forward would be courage. While I might not be seen as bold to my contemporaries - possibly a type B vs a type A personality - having the courage to take the first step or trust my gut intuition has benefitted me well. Strength can be found in taking a stance and leading. By not over-thinking things and balancing logic with emotion in decision-making, we can flex our courage muscles.

In many instances, **courage** is trusting that you need to make a career move or that a positive mindset is more important than engaging in office politics. Courage is making decisions that work and caring less about what others think of you if it is right for the organization.

The third trait would be **leading through listening**. In my case, it was not necessarily becoming a leader of a huge group of people, rather being able to exert influence and impact the things I cared about or undertook. Leading through listening did this mostly by making things a win/win by understanding other people's needs and moving toward a goal based on a shared mission. Some examples are starting a group at work for a common cause such as setting up a gym or persuading friends or a team of people to help me create events to fundraise for causes I cared about. Listening and this type of collaborative leadership carried with it a type of can-do grit.

One thing I learned early on in my career is that it doesn't matter what your title is or if you have the resources to accomplish a big goal. Sometimes it is important to just get started. Even as an entry-level manager, I was making leadership decisions because a "real leader" can make an impact without a title, such as handling customer service issues, pitching and executing winning digital campaign ideas, and collaborating on ideas to grow audiences by starting new product lines. Early in my career in my 20s, I began developing thinking out of the box and growing these EQ skills. Outside of work, I also started volunteering for community non-profit boards to make a difference and also make an impact while building valuable leadership skills.

If you were to classify your three top traits/skills into a group what would you call them? Are your top skills inherent or can they be learned?

Let's dig in and discover more about this question. In my case, the developed behaviors fall under the area of **emotional intelligence (EQ), a type of social emotional learning.**

Emotional intelligence is characterized and defined in the Oxford Dictionary as "the capacity to be aware of, control, and express one's emotions, and to handle interpersonal relationships judiciously and empathetically; emotional intelligence is the key to both personal and professional success."

It is interesting to note that these EQ skills are defined as the key to both personal and professional success.

According to Daniel Goleman, an American psychologist who helped to popularize emotional intelligence, there are five key elements to it:

- Self-awareness
- Self-regulation
- Motivation
- Empathy
- Social skills

As you look back to the start of your career, if you're like me, you may have put in long hours and rolled up your sleeves. Working on research, plans, budgets, presenting strategies, and more. During these early years in the workforce, we learn how to better develop our skills and hone in on ways to grow our foundational talents. I purport that by employing self-awareness and consciously lining up thoughts, feelings, and desires we can better attain our goals, the outcomes of our work, and improve our interactions.

In my experience, achieving the winning outcomes of doubling web audience growth or launching new sales channels helped propel other successes and earned workplace credibility. In specific jobs, a lot of the growth of the direct sales happened by carefully listening to customer feedback and tracking and analyzing purchasing patterns. Throughout the process of decision-making and flexing our judgment muscles, we can develop a sense of authentic leadership. Especially when we have a track record of success by listening to our intuition.

According to an article published by the Center for Growth, "Being your true authentic self means what you say in life aligns with what your actions. Your authentic self goes beyond what you do for a living, what possessions you own, or who you are to someone (mom, brother, girlfriend). It is who you are at your deepest core."

This definition of authenticity is what I credit a lot of the promotion in my career growth to. It includes sharing honestly when there are doubts, looking at things with optimism, and doing what it takes to succeed by going the extra mile.

Chapter 15: **Renee Lopez-Cantera**

Being your authentic self and "likeability" are important in both career and personal life. Leaders can't be robots, they have to have a human side and an empathetic side. For example, only posting that everything is perfect on social media and expecting that people will sincerely think it is your reality can end up hurting your likeability. Being your most authentic self is important in choosing friendships, making the most of family life, and taking up hobbies. For me, choosing to be in alignment with my true self has come down to choices, such as the things I choose to eat and drink, carving out time for exercise, prayer, and meditation. These conscious choices have all been part of creating a positive mindset.

Regarding authenticity, one tip I picked up was to think about feelings and process them at home and not necessarily have an immediate response or answer right away in front of colleagues or clients. Taking time to hear the still voice and respond when you might be ready to address them in a diplomatic or professional manner. Blurting out the first thing that comes to mind isn't necessarily the best way to handle things. This includes ruminating or letting your mind go places where you are actively thinking negative things about anyone. 93% of communication is non-verbal, according to Dr. Albert Mehrabian, professor emeritus of psychology at the University of California, LA. Because of this finding, your thoughts can become transparent to your clients, supervisors, and co-workers. People often make facial cues that share their true thoughts. It's good to think and be transparent, but thinking negatively about a colleague or client won't help you in a service business. So, my advice is not to let your clients or colleagues catch you off-guard when your emotions take over.

Motivation and How It Impacts Growth

Motivation is another part of emotional intelligence, and creating the energy or desire to complete tasks and achieve goals is a key ingredient. It is also important to ignite that desire along with the physical and mental capacity to see through goals and foster creativity and problem-solve.

I believe that the world needs more impassioned leaders who care about our community, our neighbors, and our environment. Of course, in business, we care about the bottom line, but now many boards are expanding to include women's voices and collaborative skills emphasizing more soft skills and a less cutthroat approach? When I first started out in the workplace in my 20s, I wasn't a skilled pro yet. However, I did start learning to trust my intuition and have the confidence to speak up for ideas I thought were winners. Also, it is important to not be afraid of failing, especially with small decisions. There is no need to be a perfectionist when you can always test and adjust courses easily, especially in the digital marketing field.

Why are increasing EQ skills and employing a positive motivational mindset so important in business? How are these skills even taught? Back in the 1990s, this wasn't even a topic taught at my business school. Currently and in recent decades, experts and leaders shared that it has been the secret to their success and there is a plethora of information and sources discussing this topic.

Oprah interviewed Daniel Goleman about this topic on an episode of Super Soul Sunday. In his 1995 best-seller, New York Times science reporter Daniel Goleman identified emotional intelligence and the brain's ability to regulate emotions as a key to a child's success in adulthood. "Children who practice mindfulness meditation at a young age," Goleman said, "Are more likely to become healthy, financially successful adults." Here, the pioneering author explained how having greater cognitive control and mastery of your emotions as a kid translates into happier adulthood.

Tuning into Empathy Can Help Drive Consultative Sales Careers

How can we tune into guidance and good decision-making? Several organizations online and through the educational system are tapping into just that.

Research has shown that empathy is the most difficult and valuable sales skill to acquire. According to Nick Kane, who blogs on this topic for his performance coaching business, "Empathy is important in one's job. The Center for Creative Leadership surveyed over 6,700 business leaders in 38 countries and found that the majority agreed empathy correlates to job performance and having more empathy equates to better performance."

Consultative selling requires deep listening and keeping the customer's requests and goals at the top of your mind.

Increasingly, companies and individuals are seeing results and the neurologic connection between EQ and other types of benefits that mindfulness brings. Google and the Huffington Post have mindfulness programs for their employees. Mindvalley is an online learning platform that has a mission to "unite the world by teaching wisdom and transformational ideas that our education system ignores."

The Masterclass platform is where anyone can access tutorials and lectures pre-recorded by experts in various fields. Masterclass wrote an article in February 2020 on "How to Use Empathy to Negotiate: 3 Types of Empathy."

These types of programs, courses, and articles show that learning about the different forms of empathy and social intelligence can help you better understand the decision-making process and motives of the people around you. For anyone in business, applying basic social psychology and learning how to be strategically empathetic can pay dividends over the course of a negotiation.

Mindset

In my opinion, mindset is the number one factor between success and failure.

According to Positive Psychology, "Positive thinking is a mental and emotional attitude that focuses on the bright side of life and expects positive results."

Expecting a winning outcome is more than half the battle. Of course, you have to put in the work and effort, but trying new things or winning new accounts often depends on your confidence and certainty that it will happen.

In the working environment, there are several goals to achieve, and drumming up the positive mindset and motivation to succeed can be a challenge at certain moments in your life. This is what separates stagnant employees from people who are thriving in their careers.

Chapter 15: **Renee Lopez-Cantera**

There are many life coaches and speakers that not only coach on performance but really hone in on mindset. Sayings such as "failure is not an option" or "no zero days" are trending in the hashtag vernacular. One of my favorite leaders in this space is Jesse Itzler. He has a coaching business called Build your Life Resume. Of course, you need credibility in the workplace, but the more interesting you make your life, the more people will gravitate to you. If you succeed on your life path, you will generate additional passion and desire to create and succeed in the workplace. Itzler trained with Navy Seals and learned through training for ultra marathons and owning several businesses about how important dedication and the mindset to win could make an impact.

Personally, I've run eight marathons and half marathons throughout my 30s and 40s. While some people don't decide to tackle these types of challenges that are outside of our comfort zones due to obstacles, why did I have the stamina and courage to plan a training process, carve out the time, and see the race through? Why did I even want to? Much was internal motivation. What motivates you to take on challenges?

These thoughts about will and desire beg the question about how people create goals and why some go with the flow and not carve a path of goals. Let's talk more about goal setting and success.

Success Patterns & Goal Setting

Companies that encourage creativity and hyper-growth have other processes for creativity and growth. In November 2017, The Atlantic published an article titled "Google X and the Science of Radical Creativity." The article addresses how at X, the so-called moonshot factory at Alphabet, the parent company of Google, they dream up far-out answers to crucial problems.

They have a team and process for creating success. They create "moonshot goals." Sometimes they are over-reaching but if you are able to get to 80% of them, they are huge wins. This goes with my adage that you don't have to be a perfectionist. Just shoot for a goal and go for it!

On a personal level, do you create moonshot goals? One of mine was to write a book. So, here I am becoming an author for the first time. My sincere desire is that something in this chapter resonates with you, or you find a resource and dive into this area. Participating in this wonderful book of women business leaders was a way to get my feet wet. Taking the step of writing this chapter has propelled me to set a goal of writing a longer book I recently started. It will have more of a spiritual tone regarding intuition.

By listening to our deepest internal desires and soul wishes for our highest self, we can create our own career path that is uniquely and perfectly tailored to our own skills and gifts and has the highest resonance to help others.

I encourage you to take online assessments and map out a path that fulfills you with goals and milestones along the way. Tests such as Myers Briggs are common. Another test is StrengthFinders, one I took with the Commonwealth Institute, a women's leadership organization that encourages and supports entrepreneurship and executive growth. I encourage you to look into these types of tests so you can uncover your personality strengths and patterns, which will hopefully lead to ways you can best utilize the skills in your wheelhouse. It's always good to know your strengths so you can further concentrate in those areas.

I also took a Value Assessment by John De Martini which I found very interesting. His major tenant is to prioritize things you are good at and delegate areas you don't enjoy as much.

My top areas to focus on were Spiritual, Business, and Family. I try to focus most endeavors in these areas to keep my level of enjoyment and engagement up and prevent burnout. Obviously, every individual or company can't afford to delegate certain undesirable tasks, but if you focus on what you love to do, you'll have less dissonance and have the energy to really make things happen.

How EQ and a Positive Mindset Helped Me Transition to Sales Leader

I transitioned into being a salesperson in my 40s after working for 15 years in marketing and branding and direct sales via written communication. At first, a bit of fear crept up going into a somewhat different role involving in-person sales where I didn't think of myself as a typical "salesperson" or a high-pressure closer.

Luckily, the empathy I had developed, my belief in a good product or service, and truly wanting to help my clients succeed, has served me well and helped to reach some difficult goals without official and prior sales training except for one Dale Carnegie course taken decades ago.

Employing a consultative approach and seeing myself as someone providing a real service or being of service made all the difference. High ticket salespeople definitely can learn from the masters in sales, but for me the developed and innate characteristics of listening, caring, courage, empathy, and confidence have made the difference in my current career. The development of EQ and the positive mindset to win has helped me and the divisions of companies I've worked with grow exponentially.

Want to propel your Career Path? Consider Hiring a Business Coach or EQ Mentor

Even though it may seem a bit expensive or premature, consider hiring someone to assist you before you have a certain level of responsibility in an organization. Hiring a business coach was something that really helped propel me in growing a business. Find someone you can share with and bounce ideas off of, who can help you map out a career path and hold you accountable. Over the years, I had Pamela, a wonderful coach who helped me for over 15 years. When I asked her for a recommendation on LinkedIn she said, "Renee puts her heart and soul and mind into everything she does." This was the ultimate compliment for someone like me on the EQ path.

Additionally, recently I have engaged with an emotional intelligence coach who has motivated me to work in ways that are a bit outside of the regular career path. Why? Because our talents and gifts can be used for a higher purpose. The work I've started with Monica Coronel has proven very valuable because of the alignment of authenticity she has brought to me. Have you heard the saying "the teacher will appear when the student is ready"? Monica's message is that you don't have to wait for a huge wake-up call to move in the direction your soul is calling you to. She has dedicated her life to fulfilling her purpose, which she defines as "assisting other people to develop/cultivate the capacity to combine reasoning/thinking and awareness/feeling to live a purposeful life!"

So, What is Your Life Purpose?

My message is to listen to your true calling, not just the one that will help you in the material world. Even though it can be a bit scary at first, you will be able to accomplish more and have resources available when your truest life path is in alignment with your deepest desires.

Of course, we all want to be paid well for the work we do. When we trust that when we tap into the multiplying effect of doing something that is part of our truest and highest calling, we will reap the highest rewards. This internal motivation is powered by your EQ, so my hope for you is that you find out what truly moves and drives YOU!

CHAPTER 16

THE BIG THREE OF WORKPLACE SUCCESS: DIFFERENCES, DIVERSITY, AND DECENCY

By **RITA KAKATI-SHAH**

Being Different

Ever since I can remember, I've been different. The way I think, how I respond, my fearlessness, and how I immerse myself in different scenarios. As a young girl, I felt out of place, but as I grew up, I realized these differences actually make me unique and shaped me into who I am today. As children, you are not taught to recognize differences in skin tone. Indeed, the first time I noticed I was darker than others was at school, when my friends called me names.

Did these experiences scar me? Absolutely. But they also taught me to survive, and over time, survival turned into acceptance. I developed an outer armor early on and became more resilient. I also learned to listen and be empathetic. Rather than cave into a downward spiral of name-calling, I adjusted, befriended, and educated others about who I was. I learned from a young age to adapt, fit in, and get along with others who didn't think the same way I did.

I was regarded as being different first because of my brown skin, then because I was a woman, and later as a mother looking to explore professional opportunities when I had a career gap to justify on my résumé. I know I am not alone, many others are also confronted for being a different skin color, gender, religion, and many other things.

Of the billions of us who have been characterized as "different" in one form or another, we have two choices: attempt to disguise or minimize our differences, or as I did throughout my life, embrace being different. I believe it is our differences that make us who we are.

Learning to embrace and celebrate being different opened a window in my universe which gave me an abundance of perspectives, thoughts, and ideas which became the foundation of my life and my career. It was those experiences that guided me through the early phases of my career. It guided me in the early 2000s as one of the very few women on the trading floor of Goldman Sachs in London, then as I negotiated deals in male-only boardrooms in the clinical trial industry, and then when I became a mother and learned how to balance the seemingly incompatible objectives of motherhood and work. And again, it was there to guide me through the launch of my company, Uma, an empowerment platform derived around diversity and inclusion principles for women and minorities to gain unshakable confidence, be poised for success, and unlock their leadership potential.

Diversity

When I was about to apply for my first job experience in my teens, my parents had a conversation with me about being different. In simple terms, there are white people, and then there is everyone else. There are men, and then there is everyone else. I was part of the "everyone else" category. This conversation shaped my formative years. It paved the path for me to treat and educate others on

Chapter 16: **Rita Kakati-Shah**

differences, similarities, and how they treat others. To understand that every life experience is valuable, and no matter what color, race, culture, gender, or life situation, everyone should be celebrated as being unique and powerful.

The concepts of diversity, inclusion, and equality in the workplace, although immensely powerful, can also be a source of divisiveness and conflict, which creates an atmosphere of tension and bickering. Diversity in itself aims to "invite" people from minority backgrounds to take part – such as women and people of color. However, as a woman of color, I never want to feel like I have been given a job opportunity just because I checked both the woman and ethnic minority boxes. Rather, I want to be hired due to my credentials, professional experiences, and most importantly, my diversity of thought. Ironically, by not delving deeper and finding people who have diverse experiences, opinions, or frames of reference, we may actually be masking organizational groupthink and creating intolerance.

It wasn't until I started my career in finance that I could really apply my experiences of diversity and being different at work. As one of the very few women on the equities trading floor at Goldman Sachs, I initially wondered where all the women were. I wanted to ask them about their careers, see what they did day to day, and also have them come and see what I do. Back then, the "Women's Network" did exist in London, but had a reputation of just being women meeting for coffee, and there wasn't any professional networking or career development association with the group. I attended several of the coffee meetings, and after sharing numerous ideas and plans, we managed to change the face of the Women's Network so much that I was tasked with creating a cross-divisional footprint, which would later serve as the foundation for other European locations. In a similar vein, after congregating and joining forces with like-minded colleagues from different divisions in London, we put together a pitch to senior leadership, which later led to the successful formation of the Asian Professionals' Network.

Diversity is about bringing together different people and everyone adapting and learning from our colleagues' experiences in order to work together as a team to increase output, efficiency, and, ultimately, shareholder value. The conversation around diversity, inclusion, and equity in the workplace is a major test of leadership among CEOs and other business executives in the corporate world.

Decency

In the early 2000s in finance, the most critical leadership quality we were measured against was IQ (Intelligence Quotient). As I progressed into the next decade, it was our EQ (Emotional Quotient) that became the prime focus. Although these are indeed key attributes in leadership development, the one trait that encapsulates all of the people-friendly qualities that your employees, clients, and shareholders look for in their leaders boils down to one thing: whether or not you are a decent person.

The concept of a Decency Quotient (DQ) is twofold. First, employees seek this from their workplace and leadership to ultimately base their career decisions off. It is what attracts employees to want to join a company, and ultimately what leads them to want to stay. Secondly, from a leadership perspective, having a high DQ focuses your attention on having a genuine desire in doing right by others. It is ultimately the evolution of your IQ and EQ, and also factors in key measurements of honesty, kindness, and integrity.

Chapter 16: **Rita Kakati-Shah**

For today's leaders, attributes such as empathy, listening skills, emotional intelligence, and decency are more critical than ever. They must be exercised like a muscle, practiced and cultivated every day. These skills are crucial in managing and navigating the intricate issues of differing opinions, cultures, and emotions. As I have said so frequently in my talks around the world, to truly strive for diversity, inclusion, and equity in the workforce, decency has to be at its heart. Decency is the differentiator, and as a concept is simple, concise, and universal.

With the growing presence and economic power of women, the workplace of today is one of new attitudes, new concerns, and new expectations. And the person who leads them must have the right set of intrapersonal and interpersonal skills to do so.

Thus, Decency Quotient is getting more recognition. Whether from the CEO of Mastercard, Ajay Banga, or the Dean of the Fuqua School of Business at Duke University, Bill Boulding, decency is being recognized as the missing cog of three critical attributes for workers and leaders, namely IQ, EQ, and DQ.

Today, the premium is not on organizational management, but people management. Taking a talented, highly motivated, diverse workforce and blending them into high-performance teams that challenge, collaborate, and innovate. Their motivation, feeling like they belong, are valued, challenged, understood, and compensated fairly commensurate with their value. These are the secrets of leadership success today, which can be simplified into a basic human quality that resides in us all, the Decency Quotient.

CHAPTER 17

ENCOURAGING THE NEXT GENERATION OF FEMALE TECHNOLOGY LEADERS

By **SHANNON WILKINSON**

Since the beginning of my career, I have been in the technology industry. For the last six years, I have been in cybersecurity. I am also a wife and mother. To some, I am a mythical, magical creature with the moniker of "Woman in a Male-Dominated Industry" or "momtrepreneur" as a female cybersecurity founder.

Over the past several years, I have spoken at conferences about being a woman in technology or cybersecurity and being female in a male-dominated industry. This, along with experiences mentoring a few young adults, has allowed me to pursue my mission of supporting and encouraging the next generation of technology leaders, especially females who are greatly underrepresented, particularly in the cybersecurity industry. I also have three young daughters, who are heavily interested in technology. With a gentle nudge from my husband to put my passion and thoughts down on paper, I recently wrote a book titled *Ripping off the Hoodie - Encouraging the Next Generation of Girls in STEM,* which explores the unconscious bias, conscious bias, harassment, discrimination, and societal pressures facing girls and women in STEM (Science, Technology, Engineering, and Mathematics) and why having more girls involved is crucial for the future of innovation.

One day, likely not in my lifetime but perhaps in my daughters, I would love for women in technology simply to be considered experts in their fields rather than female experts in the field. What I am advocating and hoping for in the future is for people to stop looking at me as a woman in cybersecurity and just look at me as a cybersecurity expert, irrespective of my gender. I believe this will become a reality as more girls pursue education and careers in technology, but they will not do that without the support of their educators, mentors, and perhaps most importantly, their families.

While women make up 47 percent of the workforce in the U.S., they only comprise 24 percent of the workers in the technology industry[1]. Surprisingly, technology is the only STEM industry where the percentage of women participating has fallen in the past 20 years[2]. When you look at cybersecurity, the number of women in the field recently jumped up to 24 percent[3] from 11 percent in 2017[4]. I am thrilled there has been progress, but there is still a great deal of room for improvement. One common misconception I have faced when talking about more gender diversity within technology and cybersecurity is that some believe that what I am seeking is a 50/50 split of men and women in the industry. While that would truly be an incredible achievement, what I would truly like to see is more involvement in females in the field of technology, perhaps into the low 40th percentile, wage equality, and reducing the amount of discrimination and harassment women in technology face. The first can be solved by encouraging interest in STEM in young girls and continuing to support them, either as parents, educators, or mentors as they progress through their studies and career. The latter two will take a change in culture and procedures at the organizational level.

It is important to note that the challenge of gender diversity within technology is not limited to the United States. While the U.S. has made strides toward more inclusion, other countries are also working on increasing their gender diversity. If you research girls in technology or women in technology in the news, you will find a plethora of articles and studies from around the world that are analyzing the effects and benefits of employing diverse workforces as well as the challenges countries are facing in moving the needle toward more diversity. For instance, Germany has less than a 17 percent female technology workforce[5], and Japan, a country known for contributing to advances in technology, has less than a 15 percent female technical workforce[6]. Japan also is struggling to overcome a significant pay gap between genders, as women make up to 30 percent less than their male colleagues in the same roles.

Promoting gender diversity in technology is not only a good idea because it is the right thing to do, but it also comes with real positive economic impacts. According to McKinsey & Company, companies with gender diversity are 15 percent more likely to earn more than their competitors[7] and having more women in the workforce could increase the global GDP by 26 percent[8]. There is even evidence that having more women working in an industry boosts the wages of men working in the same industry[9]. This boost in wages is due in part to a rise in productivity, which in turn increases the growth of the company. In addition to growth and productivity gains, organizations also gain more unique solutions by employing a diverse workforce. Women bring different perspectives and often employ distinct approaches to solving problems than their male counterparts. In the technology field, this results in "general collective intelligence," increasing performance and resulting in more creativity in research and development as well as applications of technology. All of these factors show that diversity makes organizations perform better.

Yet despite the many proven benefits of gender-diverse workforces, women are pushed away from careers in technology by a variety of factors, often starting at a young age. In the 1990s, a study was published that said that girls do not perform as well as boys in science and mathematics[10]. However, more recent studies show that both genders score almost identically in science and math assessments (although girls do perform slightly better in arts[11]). The incorrect perception that girls somehow are inferior in STEM subjects results in both girls and sometimes their parents pushing them away from technology studies, starting as early as middle school. A study by Microsoft found that girls who are encouraged and supported by their parents to pursue STEM subjects are twice as likely to continue in their studies and toward a career in the field[12]. Some might be surprised to learn that more girls than boys earn credits in algebra, pre-calculus, advanced biology, chemistry, and health science/technologies in high school. Yet things change a bit when we look to the university-level. Of the bachelor's degrees awarded in the U.S., females account for 58 percent of the total, however, only 36 percent of STEM degrees go to women[13].

Lastly, there is the issue of sexual harassment and discrimination, where over one-third of employees within the technology industry have either witnessed or experienced sexism[14] in the workplace, which has tarnished the reputation of the industry and drives girls and women away.

As the mother of three inquisitive and technology-inclined daughters, I have faced challenges in satisfying their desire for

Chapter 17: **Shannon Wilkinson**

technology-themed clothing and toys designed for girls. My daughters absolutely loathe having to shop in the boy's section of the store for video game-themed t-shirts. They also would much rather have a science kit that would create an explosion, the bigger the better, rather than make bath bombs. Clothing makers seem to think that my daughters should only be interested in narwhals, mermaids, unicorns, kittens, and a variety of other cute, cuddly animals, whereas boy's clothing is promoting sports, technology, and adventure. While there are some science/technology themed toys for the girls, such as Project MC™ and Mattel's Barbie™ "You Can Be Anything" line, as a parent, it has still been difficult to provide toys specifically designed for girls interested in technology and robotics without venturing into a section designated for boys. It seems that as a society, we still unconsciously (or purposefully) push girls away from science and technology while encouraging the interest with boys and this will continue to cause issues in the future. Perhaps a real solution is to stop gendering toys at all and have all dolls, science kits, and toys be for any gender instead of making one pink and another blue.

You may wonder what kind of issues steering girls away from technology will cause in the future. Today, more companies than ever are looking for employees with technological skill sets. In fact, eight in ten positions in 2017 required digital skills[15], which means performing tasks on computers such as using spreadsheets, word processors, and being able to easily use other software programs. There is also a greater need for advanced technical skill sets, such as computer programming. While technology companies still employ a majority of tech employees, there is increasing demand across all industries as companies seek to develop competitive advantages through the use of technology. Over 60 percent of the new jobs created in the past ten years has required medium-to-advanced technical skills[16], which means if girls continue not to choose STEM education and careers, then they will lack the skill sets needed to find positions and succeed in the workplace.

There are significant skills gaps developing in new fields such as artificial intelligence, robotics, and machine learning to name a few. These new fields are also resulting in a reduction of other jobs as technology advances. Look at the advances in robotics and automation; think to your local retail stores and you will realize that more and more cash registers are going to self-service with one attendant supervising five or more checkout areas. Fast food restaurants are creating self-service kiosks and launching mobile apps that allow a customer to place an order from home for pickup or delivery, eliminating the need for order takers and cashiers. A McKinsey Global Institute study estimated that up to 30 percent of job tasks can be automated and 60 percent of occupations, especially more routine jobs, could be replaced by automation[17]. Machines are replacing certain jobs, and companies are continuing to innovate and utilize technology for efficiency and cost savings. The caveat to this is that someone needs to know how to create the technology, implement it, and maintain and oversee it, so with the elimination of certain positions, new ones have been created that require more technical skills.

Looking at my own industry and the skills gap, the gap within cybersecurity has worsened for the fourth straight year in a row, and it is estimated that there are over four million unfilled jobs[18] due to a lack of available cybersecurity professionals. There simply are just not enough people with the correct skillset to fill the open positions. The skills gap has developed over time due to a lack of training and education opportunities, the ever-changing threat landscape, the inability to establish a work/life balance, and organizations not focusing on providing adequate budgets for cybersecurity. It has been said that in cybersecurity there is a zero percent unemployment rate as there are so many vacant positions available, but in order to close the skills gap, a growth of 145 percent is required to completely close the gap, which simply is not realistic. But as the saying goes, we can do better. So, I am doing all I can to encourage the next generation of cybersecurity leaders by speaking to groups of middle and high school students about opportunities in technology and making myself available to mentor those who are studying or starting out their careers. Sharing career information and advice, mentoring, and sponsoring technical groups are just a few things that technology professionals can do to help work toward closing both the skills and gender gaps.

How far we will get in closing the skills gap in the future remains to be seen but we must work to close the gap and encourage future generations to develop technical skills. We will not be able to solve the skills gap by just encouraging boys to go into STEM careers and we cannot just focus on one subset of skills such as coding classes. We need to engage, encourage, and mentor both girls and boys to explore the possibilities of technology education and careers and make them aware of the immense possibilities to contribute to the future of innovation.

---

[1] Sarah K. White, "Women in Tech Statistics: The Hard Truths of an Uphill Battle," CIO (CIO, January 23, 2020), https://www.cio.com/article/3516012/women-in-tech-statistics-the-hard-truths-of-an-uphill-battle.html.

[2] Aaron Price, "Why Gender Diversity In Tech Matters," Entrepreneur, February 28, 2017, https://www.entrepreneur.com/article/289293.

3 "(ISC)² Cybersecurity Workforce Study: Women in Cybersecurity", Cybersecurity and IT Security Certifications and Training (ISC)², 2019), https://www.isc2.org/Research/Women-in-Cybersecurity.

4 Laura Paine, "New Research: In 2017, Women Still Only Make Up 11 Percent of the Cybersecurity Workforce," Veracode, March 23, 2017, https://www.veracode.com/blog/new-research-2017-women-still-only-make-11-percent-cybersecurity-workforce.

5 Stefan Kingham, "Women in Tech: How Does Germany Compare to the Rest of Europe?," Women in Tech: How does Germany compare to the rest of Europe?, March 29, 2018, https://blog.honeypot.io/women-in-tech-germany/.

6 Georgina Varley, "Women in Tech by Country," Women of Silicon Roundabout Conference 2020 (Ascend Global Media, November 21, 2018), https://www.women-in-technology.com/wintec-blog/women-in-tech-by-country.

7 Vivian Hunt, Dennis Layton, and Sara Prince, "Why Diversity Matters," February 14, 2020, https://www.mckinsey.com/business-functions/organization/our-insights/why-diversity-matters.

8 Jonathan Woetzel et al., "How Advancing Women's Equality Can Add $12 Trillion to Global Growth," McKinsey & Company (McKinsey & Company, July 4, 2019), https://www.mckinsey.com/featured-insights/employment-and-growth/how-advancing-womens-equality-can-add-12-trillion-to-global-growth.

9 Christine Lagarde and Jonathan D Ostry, "The Macroeconomic Benefits of Gender Diversity," VOX, CEPR Policy Portal, December 5, 2018, https://voxeu.org/article/macroeconomic-benefits-gender-diversity.

10 Paglin, Morton, and Anthony M. Rufolo. "Heterogeneous Human Capital, Occupational Choice, and Male-Female Earnings Differences." Journal of Labor Economics 8, no. 1 (1990): 123-44. www.jstor.org/stable/2535301.

11 Silvia Griselda PhD student and Rigissa Megalokonomou Lecturer in Economics, "Girls Score the Same in Maths and Science as Boys, but Higher in Arts – This May Be Why They Are Less Likely to Pick STEM Careers," The Conversation, June 18, 2020, https://theconversation.com/girls-score-the-same-in-maths-and-science-as-boys-but-higher-in-arts-this-may-be-why-they-are-less-likely-to-pick-stem-careers-131563.

12 Suzanne Choney, "Why Do Girls Lose Interest in STEM? New Research Has Some Answers - and What We Can Do about It," Stories (Microsoft, March 13, 2018), https://news.microsoft.com/features/why-do-girls-lose-interest-in-stem-new-research-has-some-answers-and-what-we-can-do-about-it/.

Chapter 17: **Shannon Wilkinson**

[13] "Science, Technology, Engineering, and Mathematics (STEM) Education, by Gender," National Center for Education Statistics (NCES) (U.S. Department of Education, 2019), https://nces.ed.gov/fastfacts/display.asp?id=899.

[14] Leah Dunlevy, "More Than a Third of Tech Industry Employees Have Experienced or Witnessed Sexism, a New Survey Finds," Pacific Standard, April 25, 2019, https://psmag.com/news/sexism-in-the-tech-industry.

[15] Scott Bittle, "Digital Skills Gap: Middle-Skill Jobs, Digital Literacy, and Future of Work," Burning Glass Technologies, September 2017, https://www.burning-glass.com/research-project/digital-skills-gap/.

[16] Edward Alden and Laura Taylor-Kale, "Findings I Future U.S. Workforce Calls for More Technology Skills," Council on Foreign Relations (Council on Foreign Relations, April 2018), https://www.cfr.org/report/the-work-ahead/report/findings.html.

[17] James Manyika, "Technology, Jobs, and the Future of Work," McKinsey & Company (McKinsey & Company, May 24, 2017), https://www.mckinsey.com/featured-insights/employment-and-growth/technology-jobs-and-the-future-of-work.

[18] Help Net Security November 8, "Cybersecurity Workforce Skills Gap Rises to over 4 Million," Help Net Security, November 8, 2019, https://www.helpnetsecurity.com/2019/11/08/cybersecurity-workforce-skills-gap/.

CHAPTER 18

WOMEN IN BUSINESS: EMOTIONAL INTELLIGENCE IS THE UNDERRATED SKILL OF SUCCESS

By **VICTORIA SOSA**

How many times have we seen success determined by test scores and numbers? Yet this is only a two-dimensional view of success and other factors that can make someone succeed in work, school, personal relationships, and more. Over the past ten years, as I have learned and grown, I began to see how the root of success for me has been in the strength of my business relationships and interpersonal skills. I'll never forget one of my professors at UNC-Chapel Hill, Dr. Steve May, who taught interpersonal communication. He said that when we graduate and go to interview for jobs, the person interviewing you isn't looking at just your GPA and degree, they are looking to see if they like you and want to work with you. I know, engage mind being blown! Wait, so everything we were taught about testing and GPAs was not going to land me my dream job? Or going to one of the top universities in the country would not guarantee me a job at the best companies? This began an interesting conversation about interpersonal skills and emotional intelligence that I wanted to understand and learn more about. It completely flipped my idea of how to be successful upside down. Why wasn't an emphasis on communication and interpersonal skills taught in school alongside algebra and literature?

I am in sales and marketing, and know how important relationships are to be successful - but is this an innate skill or can it be learned? I've realized over time this is a skill you can learn and improve upon to be a top performer and leader in any area of your life. If someone does not enjoy working with you, they are not going to buy from you, refer business to you, or wish to work with you. Now, will everyone like you? NO! That is one of the biggest obstacles I had to understand. You cannot make everyone happy and not everyone is going to like you, but if you attempt to communicate as they do, truly practice active listening, and read subtle body language, you can create a better relationship.

What is Emotional Intelligence?

Some people have never even heard of emotional intelligence, as it is a somewhat newer discovery, as of the mid-1970s to early 1980s to be exact, but it has become a must-have skill in business. Emotional Intelligence, also known as EQ, was first coined by Wayne Payne for a doctoral dissertation and was defined as "the subset of social intelligence that involves the ability to monitor one's own and others' feelings and emotions, to discriminate among them, and to use this information to guide one's thinking and actions." Later, psychologists Peter Salovey from Yale University and John D. Mayer from the University of New Hampshire published an article entitled "Emotional Intelligence" and explained what it is and how it can be used to help us grow as people and in business.

Emotional intelligence is defined as an ability, versus your intelligence quotient (IQ), which is a score derived from a collection of tests and assessments to measure your level of intelligence. Even the difference in verbiage shows how emotional intelligence is more than an arbitrary number from a test score. It is an action or talent that

Chapter 18: **Victoria Sosa**

can be learned and improved. I began noticing while in college how important self-awareness is and how this skill was helping me at my job as a part-time leasing consultant. I used to say to myself, "I will never be in sales!" I had this idea that salespeople were just pushy, aggressive, and shallow. In my mind, a career in sales or marketing was like a car salesman. An aggressive, pushy salesman was not what I envisioned myself to be. Yet, I was in sales at an apartment community, and I was really good at it and I enjoyed it. When you're in your early twenties, it's hard to know what you want to do until you've experienced it. I was studying to be a speech pathologist at the time. Yet in working this part-time summer job while in school, I made a miraculous discovery that would help me in my career and overall success: I enjoyed building relationships and refining my communication skills to help people find a place to live.

After graduating from college, I continued working with the same company and was offered the Sales and Marketing Manager position. In this role, I learned more about how to educate people about products or services and refine certain skills. With emotional intelligence, there are different actions that help you practice this effectively. Emotional intelligence is more than just noticing how someone speaks or looking at their body language. It consists of social awareness and competence, empathy, emotional regulation, and self-awareness.

Implementing Emotional Intelligence

In my experience, social awareness and competence are beneficial when working with a client or customer, especially if you want to persuade them on why they need to choose you over the competition. In North Carolina, we have a lot of people moving from out of state. Many are coming from the northeast like New York or

Massachusetts. In the south, we tend to talk a little more slowly and not be as pushy as people from New England may be more accustomed to. To be truly effective, you need to know who you are talking to and where they are from, and then subtly match their speaking style and body language. I call it being a social chameleon. I tend to code-switch, which is when you switch between different variations of your language style. National Public Radio even did an article in 2013 titled "Five Reasons Why People Code-Switch" and talks about how people do it both consciously and subconsciously. In my case, I did it subconsciously and did not even realize it was a skill you could learn or enhance. When I met with potential clients, I would match their style of language unbeknownst to myself and it would help them relax and feel more comfortable speaking with me.

Body language is crucial to understand when increasing your emotional intelligence and social competence. Body language has been studied since 1872 when Charles Darwin was discovering evolution. Body language makes up most of our communication, much more than verbal communication. I had taken a class at Duke about communicating with people from Asia and understanding their culture to help improve communication with those from other countries. In the U.S., sustained eye contact means you are listening and engaged but if you are speaking with someone from Asia, they feel that sustained eye contact can be aggressive. Certain other things to look out for in body language is how they are sitting. If they are slouched back, they are relaxed and open to what you have to say but if they have their arms crossed and lips pursed, they may be skeptical and need more time to trust you, so you would approach them with empathy and patience.

Chapter 18: **Victoria Sosa**

When practicing social awareness, I am also keeping in mind my demographic. I work with seniors over the age of 70, and for many, moving to a retirement community is scary and a big change in their lifestyle. So, I make sure to communicate with them in an empathetic and caring way. Many are scared of falling at home alone and no one being there to help them, others are resistant to change. Often, family dynamics come into play, which can make the sales process more complicated. I have seen how showing empathy in working with customers or clients allows you to look at your product or service from their perspective. When you know someone is resistant to change but that your service would help them, you have to understand their emotions or way of thinking and what is preventing them from making the decision to work with you and then educate them on your services. Educating someone versus trying to convince them of why they need your service or product builds trust and credibility. As Stephen Covey stated in his famous book *7 Habits of Highly Effective People*, "Seek first to understand, then to be understood."

When communicating with empathy, it is crucial to really listen to what your client is saying and then acknowledge their feelings. For example, I had a woman who lost her husband a year ago and was searching for options to move. She was scared of change but no longer wanted to be alone. I first acknowledged her feelings and came from a place of understanding. Then I highlighted all the positives of moving to our community and educated her on the lifestyle she could have there. So, three key points are acknowledging their feelings, turning a negative into a positive (creating hope), and educating them to increase trust and credibility. Many people are driven by their emotions when it comes to making big decisions such as taking a new job or buying a home. If you can identify their emotions and relate to them, then you create a solid foundation on which to build future business.

Lastly, we need to practice emotional regulation and self-awareness to enhance business relationships and increase sales. Emotional regulation sounds a bit daunting; if we could control every emotion, we would be like machines, and humans just do not operate that way. What I mean by emotional regulation is the ability to manage our feelings in a way that is productive instead of ineffective. You may have heard the phrases "roll with the punches" or "what doesn't kill you makes you stronger." When I hear these sayings, I think of how important resilience and the ability to bounce back from negative situations is. We will all have failures and make mistakes, but if we learn from those experiences to move forward and grow professionally and emotionally, then that, in my opinion, is the true essence of resilience. When we increase our emotional regulation, we are able to handle negative feedback and criticism in a constructive and positive way which does not hinder your performance but instead enhances it. This goes hand in hand with self-awareness, which is the ability to recognize your feelings and emotions and how they affect others. For example, I have an uplifting demeanor and I use that to create a light-hearted experience when I am working with families and potential residents since often the idea of moving for them is scary or an emotional conversation. Self-awareness also comes with time and experience. As you grow, it is important to identify your personal strong suits and be aware of those attributes and use them in your professional and personal life.

Chapter 18: **Victoria Sosa**

When looking back at the beginning of my career, I can honestly say all of these communication skills and elements of emotional intelligence have helped me become successful and I still continue to refine these skills. You should never stop learning and I hope by sharing my experiences it will allow you to become more emotionally intelligent, too. If you apply those skills to your life and career, it will not only benefit your success but also your relations with others.

CONCLUSION

By **ADAM TORRES**

Women come from many backgrounds and are involved in all levels and types of businesses. Their stories are infinitely varied. Along the way, they experience success and failure. Some of the women presented here are further along in their careers than others, but one common trait is shared among all of them: they are never done working on themselves. They continue to push forward and test the boundaries of what they are capable of. Above all, this one trait will be responsible for much of the innovation that occurs in our generation and the generations that follow. Diversity and the female perspective in business is a beautiful way to continue to learn and grow.

Thank you for reading,

Adam Torres

P.S. Don't forget to listen to our podcasts at **MissionMatters.com**

APPENDIX

Adam Torres | Foreword | Page iii
Co-Founder Mission Matters
MissionMatters.com
Instagram: @AskAdamTorres
Twitter: @AskAdamTorres

Dr. Airies Davis | Chapter 1 | Page 1
Founder and Principal Consultant, WorkforcEQi LLC
info@workforcEQi.com
Twitter: @AiriesDavis
LinkedIn: https://www.linkedin.com/in/airiesdavis/

Banu Raghuraman | Chapter 2 | Page 15
Director, Business & Process Analysis, Info-Tech Research Group
LinkedIn: https://www.linkedin.com/in/brraman/

Camilla Jeffs | Chapter 3 | Page 25
Founder & CEO, Steady Stream Investments
camilla@steadystreaminvestments.com
www.steadystreaminvestments.com
LinkedIn: https://www.linkedin.com/in/camilla-jeffs-175232103/
Instagram: Steady Stream Investments
Facebook: Steady Stream Investments

Carolyn Barth | Chapter 4 | Page 35
CEO, Digital Content Strategy LLC
Award-winning agency specializing in authority marketing, PR, and media.
LinkedIn: https://linkedin.com/in/carolynbarth
(Carolyn Barth Storytelling - 21,000 followers)
Facebook: @CarolynBarthPR
Instagram: @CarolynBarthPR
Book a 15-min. virtual coffee: https://calendly.com/carolynbarth

Claudia Romo Edelman | Chapter 5 | Page 43
Founder of We Are All Human Foundation
claudia@weareallhuman.org
Instagram: claudiaromoedelman
LinkedIn: https://www.linkedin.com/in/claudiagromo/

Cydni Tetro | Chapter 6 | Page 51
CEO Tetch XP
Founder & President of Women Tech Council
cydni@tetchxp.com
Twitter: @cydtetro
Instagram @cydtetro and @womentechcouncil
Linkedin: https://www.linkedin.com/in/cydnitetro/

Denisa Axhami | Chapter 7 | Page 61
Founder and President of The Detroit Entrepreneur
info@thedetroitentrepreneur.com
www.thedetroitentrepreneur.com

Krystalán Chryssomallis | Chapter 8 | Page 69
CMO, Yanni Works Entertainment
info@krystalan.com
Krystalan.com
Instagram: @Krystalann
Facebook: @KrystalanC
Twitter: @Krystalan_C

Dr. Lori Haddad | Chapter 9 | Page 75
CEO @ WakeUpnotMakeUp, LLC
Skin by dr. lori
lori@drlori.com
Linkedin: Lori Haddad, D.O.
Twitter: @WakeUpnotMakeUp

Marguerita Cheng | Chapter 10 | Page 85
CEO of Blue Ocean Global Wealth
Twitter: https://twitter.com/BlueOceanGW
LinkedIn: https://www.linkedin.com/in/margueritacheng/
Websites: http://margueritacheng.com/
https://www.blueoceanglobalwealth.com/

Marisa Impellizzeri | Chapter 11 | Page 95
marisaimpellizzeri.com
Director of Brand Strategy, Durable Connect
https://durableconnect.com
Director of Marketing, Home Community Center
http://homecc.org
LinkedIn: https://www.linkedin.com/in/marisaimpellizzeri/

Michelle Mekky | Chapter 12 | Page 103
President & Founder of Mekky Media Relations
michelle@mekkymedia.com
www.mekkymedia.com
Facebook: @mekkymichelle
LinkedIn: https://www.linkedin.com/in/michellemekky/
Twitter: @michellemekky
Instagram: @michelle.mekky
Facebook: @Mekky Media Relations
Twitter: @MekkyMedia
Instagram: @MekkyMedia
LinkedIn: https://www.linkedin.com/company/mekky-media-relations-inc./

Racquel Rivera | Chapter 13 | Page 113
Racquel.Rivera@Compass.com
Instagram: @RacquelRRivera
LinkedIn: https://www.linkedin.com/in/racquelrivera/
Facebook: https://www.facebook.com/RacquelRRivera/

Rani Khetarpal | Introduction, Chapter 14 | Page vii, Page 121
Vice President, Provider Innovations
New Century Health, A subsidiary of Evolent Health
Founder, Global Transitional Care
LinkedIn: https://www.linkedin.com/in/ranikhetarpal/

Renee Lopez-Cantera | Chapter 15 | Page 135
Vice President of Business Development
Eikon Digital USA
rlopez.cantera@eikondigital.com
https://www.eikonusa.com
LinkedIn: www.linkedin.com/in/reneelopez-cantera

Rita Kakati-Shah | Chapter 16 | Page 149
Founder & CEO, Uma
pr@beboldbeuma.com
Phone: +1 (212) 203-3379
www.beboldbeuma.com
Facebook: https://www.facebook.com/BeBoldBeUma/
Twitter: @BeBoldBeUma
Instagram: @BeBoldBeUma
YouTube: https://www.youtube.com/channel/UCxmtxRE1EzOD5ULLdrv6aBA
LinkedIn: https://www.linkedin.com/in/rita-kakati

Shannon Wilkinson | Chapter 17 | Page 155
CEO, Tego Cyber Inc
https://tegocyber.com
info@tegocyber.com
Facebook: @tegocyber
Twitter: @tegocyber
LinkedIn: https://www.linkedin.com/company/tegocyber
Twitter: @SWilkinsonCyber
LinkedIn: https://www.linkedin.com/in/swilkinsoncyber/

Victoria Sosa | Chapter 18 | Page 165
Marketing Director of The Cambridge at Brier Creek
Cambridge Village Optimal Living
VSosa@cvsliving.com
Facebook: @CambridgeBrierCreek
www.TheCambridgeBrierCreek.com
www.LightentheMind.com
Victoria@LightentheMind.com
Facebook: https://www.linkedin.com/in/victoria-sosa-cam-02389137/

Listen to our
PODCASTS

MISSION MATTERS
WE AMPLIFY STORIES

www.MissionMatters.com

The
PODCAST MATTERS
SCHOOL

Why Did I Start This School?

Every day, I interview business owners, entrepreneurs, and executives. I've done over 1,500 podcast episodes.

Depending on when you read this, I'll likely be over 2,000 episodes!

Many of the people I interview ask me to help them launch their own podcast. My ultimate goal is to help people spread their story and message. So, of course, I started helping people one by one. I figured that the more people I can help start podcasts, the more people I would help spread their message. Mission accomplished.

But then things got a little out of control. See, I have a habit of over-committing. It got to the point where helping people launch their own podcast was taking up more time than I had available.

So, I was faced with two choices.

One, I could tell people that I just don't have the time to help them.

Or, two, create a podcast school for those who want to launch a podcast or continue to grow their reach for an existing podcast.

I wanted to continue helping people, so the school was born.

What Makes This School Different?

First, this course is NOT designed for people looking for a way to make a quick buck.

The course is designed for busy professionals who have always wanted to start a podcast but have never had the time or knowledge to get one started. Others who will benefit from the teachings in this course are the part-time podcasters who can't quite figure out how to grow their audience.

While I'm not claiming that I've seen all podcast courses ever made, I can tell you that when I was first getting started, it seemed like all of the courses were really long and felt like part-time jobs just to complete. Well, I wasn't looking for a part-time job, I had a business already and I just wanted to podcast.

So, my commitment to you is that each lesson in this course will be straight to the point. Most videos are under five minutes and many of them are two minutes or less. Why? Because you don't need to hear me drone on. You just need the information so you can take action. Less time learning and more time in action is what will grow your podcast.

Finally, though it's kind of weird for me to say this considering I had almost 14 years of wealth management experience before going full-time into media about three years ago, but this is what I do for a living.

This is not a "side hustle" for me. I get paid to podcast, not just to teach. Why do I tell you this? Because you want to learn from someone who lives and breathes what they are teaching. You don't want someone experimenting with YOUR time.

For more information visit **MissionMatters.com**.

Happy Podcasting!

Adam Torres

OTHER AVAILABLE TITLES

In the fourth edition of *Mission Matters (Business Leaders Edition Vol 4)*, Adam Torres features 18 top professionals who share their lessons on leadership. In these pages, through inspiring stories, you'll discover:

- How patient care and technology meet in the medical field.
- How digital transformation is imperative for companies.
- What creating your dream retirement looks like.
- How to create a result-driven culture in your company.
- How to pivot your marketing to survive crisis situations.
- Why cohesion is more important than engagement in an organization.
- And much more!

Purchase at **MissionMatters.com**.

In the third edition of *Money Matters (Business Leaders Edition Vol 3)*, Adam Torres features 13 top professionals who share their lessons on leadership. In these pages, through inspiring stories, you'll discover:

- Different approaches to leadership and people management.
- Rules for success from a Green Beret.
- How to effectively manage a company full of millennial employees.
- How to transform your marketing mindset.
- Where customer success and employee success meet.
- What manifesting your success in business looks like.
- And much more.

Purchase at MissionMatters.com.

In the second edition of *Money Matters (Business Leaders Edition Vol 2)*, Adam Torres features 18 top professionals who share their lessons on leadership. In these pages, through inspiring stories, you'll discover:

- How to harness the entrepreneurial mindset.
- Why scaling your business for sustainable growth is vital.
- How to grow your eCommerce business.
- Lessons learned from sales experts.
- How to level up your leadership.
- How to manage your energy.
- And much more.

Purchase at **MissionMatters.com**.

Navigating the world of real estate can be stressful. Are you getting closer or further away from your goals?

Adam Torres is here to help you move forward. In his latest edition of *Money Matters (Real Estate Edition Volume 2)*, Torres features 13 top professionals who share their lessons in real estate.

In these pages, through inspiring stories, you'll discover:
- How to get more properties through syndication.
- How to implement servant leadership to have a more successful business.
- Why investing in real estate is not just for rich people.
- How important insurance is in real estate transactions and what to look for.
- Why using a private lender can help you in real estate transactions.
- What legal options you have to protect your assets.
- And much more!

Purchase at **MissionMatters.com**.

In the original edition of *Money Matters (Business Leaders Edition)*, Adam Torres features 15 top professionals who share their lessons on leadership. In these pages, through inspiring stories, you'll discover:

- How to create a clear path for growth.
- Why every business should act like a media company.
- How to build a community to last a lifetime.
- Lessons learned from professional soccer.
- How to maintain a well-connected brain for peak performance.
- How to create harmony through union in business.
- And much more.

Embracing diversity and inclusion in a rapidly changing business landscape can be challenging. Are you and your organization positioned properly for this new age of connectivity? Torres features fourteen top Asian leaders who share their lessons on diversity, equality and inclusion.

Navigating the world of real estate can be stressful. Are you getting closer or further from your goals? Finance guru Adam Torres is here to help you move forward. His guide, Money Matters, features 15 top professionals who share lessons from their more than 250 years of combined experience.

In this clear, concise manual, financial expert Adam Torres goes over the basics of personal finance and investing and shows you how to grow your wealth. Torres makes sure you are prepared for whatever life throws your way. It's never too early to think about the future and his book will give you the right tools to tackle it.

All books available for purchase at **MissionMatters.com**.

This workbook has been designed specifically for individuals like you who are dedicated to improving the results in all areas of your life. By following the ideas and exercises presented to you in this transformational workbook, you can move yourself into the realm of top achievers worldwide.

Download for free at **MissionMatters.com**

www.ingramcontent.com/pod-product-compliance
Lightning Source LLC
Chambersburg PA
CBHW070627220526
45466CB00001B/110